CHRIST THE CENTER

CHRIST THE CENTER

GEORGE A. F. KNIGHT

THE HANDSEL PRESS LTD
Edinburgh

WILLIAM B. EERDMANS PUBLISHING COMPANY
Grand Rapids, Michigan / Cambridge, U.K.

© Handsel Press 1999

Published jointly 1999 by
The Handsel Press Ltd
The Stables, Carberry, EH21 8PY, Scotland
and by
Wm. B. Eerdmans Publishing Co.
255 Jefferson Ave. S.E., Grand Rapids, Michigan 49503

Printed in the United States of America

03 02 01 00 99   5 4 3 2 1

British Library Cataloguing in Publication Data:

A catalogue record for this publication is available
from the British Library

Handsel ISBN 1 871828 38 4

Eerdmans ISBN 0-8028-4624-6

CONTENTS

QUOTATIONS AND CITATIONS

Frequently Hebrew and Greek words are cited in the text. Those who understand even a little Hebrew will find a wealth of insight, but for the majority of readers who do not, these words are always put in italics, and the context makes clear what the word means if it has not already been explained. The soft vowel *aleph* is written as '; the guttural *ayin* as '.

Single quotation marks are used of a word or phrase used in a special sense, or for a quote within a quote; double quotation marks are used for a literal quotation from a text.

ABBREVIATIONS

AV	Authorised Version or King James Version
BCE	Before the Common Era, common to Jews and Christians (=BC)
CE	In the Common Era, common to Jews and Christians (=AD)
CEV	Contemporary English Version
CUP	Cambridge University Press
GNB	Good News Bible or Today's English Version
HTR	Harvard Theological Review
ITC	International Theological Commentary
JB	Jerusalem Bible
JBL	Journal of Biblical Literature
LXX	Septuagint, Greek Version of the Old Testament
NAB	New American Bible
NEV	New English Version
NIV	New International Version
NRSV	New Revised Standard Version
OUP	Oxford University Press
REV	Revised English Version
RSV	Revised Standard Version
SBL	Society of Biblical Literature
SCM	Student Christian Movement
SJT	Scottish Journal of Theology
VT	Vetus Testamentum
WCC	World Council of Churches

J   Theologian responsible for parts of the Torah, about 930 BCE
D   Deuteronomy or theologian(s) who developed the Mosaic material up till about 500 BCE
P   Priestly elements in the Torah

PROLOGUE

Dwelling in a university city, as I do, I meet with cultured intellectuals from amongst both teachers and students. We may talk about the realities of life and of human existence, and find our conversation to be both stimulating and productive. Yet few of them give any place to the Incarnation of Christ in their philosophies - as my old friend since student days, the late Lesslie Newbigin might have put it, for them Christian faith is not 'public truth'.

The Old Testament anchors the whole Bible in the public arena over a long period during which the idea of Incarnation was gradually, and in many ways, being formed in the mind and heart of Israel, so that Jesus of Nazareth might in the fulness of time be presented as their Messiah and as the hope of all humankind.

I would like to thank a number of persons who carefully scrutinised the text and made many suggestions for improvement: the Rt Revd Peter Mann, the scholarly retired Anglican Bishop of Dunedin, Robert T. Walker of Edinburgh, and Jock Stein, the editor of the Handsel Press. And also my young student friend, Colin Marshall, who spent hours interpreting my hand-written script to his own satisfaction and then putting it on disk.

George A.F. Knight
Dunedin
New Zealand
May 1998

THE AUTHOR

Having completed an MA in the Classics and then advanced studies on the Semitic languages in his student days at Glasgow University, George Knight found that the Rabbis who produced the Jewish Talmud and much else had opened up for him the alternative Semitic world of thought about the Bible - 'alternative' because in many respects it is different from the philosophy of Plato and his Greek speaking successors.

For five years, in the Hitler period, the author lived in Budapest, where he sought to rehabilitate many distressed refugee Jews; this resulted frequently in deep and serious conversations. Back in Scotland, after serving as minister in two parishes, he moved to Knox College, Dunedin, where, through the teaching of Old Testament Studies, he joined in the training of men and women for the ordained ministry. After twelve years he returned to Scotand to teach at St Andrews University, and thereafter at McCormick Seminary in the USA. Finally he was called to be the founding Principal of the Pacific Theological College, Suva, Fiji. That seminary was created by the World Council of Churches to serve all the peoples of Polynesia, Melanesa, Micronesia and French Polynesia in a bi-lingual capacity. He at once made at least one year's study of Hebrew mandatory for all students!

Profesor Knight retired to live in Dunedin where he continues to edit the International Theological Commentary Series on the Old Testament. He has now written over thirty books on Jewish studies, biblical theology, Old Testament commentaries, among which these are a selection:

(1) *From Moses to Paul: a Christological Study in the Light of our Hebraic Heritage*, Lutterworth, London 1949.

(2) *A Biblical Approach to the Doctrine of the Trinity*, Oliver and Boyd, Edinburgh 1953, 1957.

(3) *A Christian Theology of the Old Testament*, SCM Press, London 1957.

(4) *Theology as Narration (Exodus)*, Eerdmans, Grand Rapids 1976.

(5) *Theology in Pictures (Genesis 1-11)*, Handsel, Edinburgh 1981.

(6) *Servant Theology (Isaiah 40-45)*, Handsel & Eerdmans, 1984.

Introduction

TWO STRANDS IN OUR HERITAGE

In the millennium before Christ, a remarkable new enlightenment, unique in character, occurred. The change was first felt in Asia but the breath of it passed over Greece and south Italy, missing out Crete, in the sixth and fifth centuries BCE. The movement was a revolt against a type of culture in which the structure of society was built upon the worship of the forces of nature, a type of polity which flourished in the archaic civilisations of Egypt and Babylonia; vestiges of it, we are told, survive in the temple cities founded in India before Aryan migration. The essence of the new movement was the recognition of an unseen world of unchanging reality behind the flux of phenomena, a spiritual universe compared with which the world of appearances seemed pale and insubstantial and came to be thought of as symbolic, or even illusory.

It is in Plato, the disciple of the Pythagoreans as well as of Socrates (probably himself the head of the Pythagorean group in Athens), that this conception of an unseen eternal world, of which the visible world is only a pale copy, gained a permanent foothold in the West about 400 BCE. What, Plato asked, if a person had eyes to see pure Beauty, undefiled by the stains of material existence: would he not hurry there, happy as a captive released from the prison cell?

According to Plato this life in Space and Time is life in a world of change whose material imperfections obscure the unchanging perfection of the eternal from most people. Only those who are specially trained to contemplate the eternal can grasp what is really important. This passing world is not to be valued or desired. What really matters is life beyond the grave.

Platonic cultures were dualistic in their philosophies: there was this life here and now, and there was real life in the beyond, after death. We call this outlook 'dualistic', first because of a belief in a world of intelligible 'Forms' or 'Ideas' existing apart from this world of tangible matter, and second because of a consequent belief that each person has an immortal soul existing in separation from the body, both before birth and after death. Some of Plato's disciples even taught that the body is a prison-house to which the soul is condemned for past misdeeds.

The ancient Hebrews, on the other hand, never accepted this dualistic world view. They saw this material world as created and affirmed by the active, righteous and steadfastly loving God who dealt with them and revealed himself to them in their life and history in this world. This life here and now was the only life to be lived before God, so they felt unable to define a separate life of the soul after the body was dead. There is hope for a life beyond, but it is not a hope for the soul alone, but for the people as a whole. This hope is glimpsed in prophecy, and sometimes linked to the coming of Messiah, or at least to some act by God in the future.

The title of this Introduction is 'The two Strands in our Heritage'. The first strand is the Hellenic, for it is our Greek background, rather than any influence of the great Asian religions, on which so much of our culture depends. The second is the Hebraic, and we find, on examination, that it stretches even further back in time.

We can date the exodus from Egypt under Moses at around 1270 BCE and thus several centuries before the rise of dualism. The Great Prophets of Israel, who developed and applied to their people's lives the heritage of Moses, were alive and active at the very period when the new philosophies of Asia and pre-Platonic Greece were coming to birth.

It would be stupid and unwise to give the impression that, in contrast to the Hebraic way of thought all is 'wrong' and unacceptable with the Hellenic world view. For example our present 'scientific' age owes much to the Greeks. The striking fact that the physical world conforms to, and so can be described by, mathematical statements, was brought out by them. Moreover, they showed the world the important of history writing. And of course the Western world appreciates the medical and surgical knowledge that Greece has given it, and the heritage of poetry, drama, art, sculpture and athletics that modern Europe and America take for granted as a legacy for the world.

Yet the emotional and physical were little esteemed; and what could be seen and touched and heard was to be valued, if at all, for the assistance it could give to the intellectual contemplation of the rational world, beyond. The view that the conception of babies had any connection with 'love' was a strange and 'unpolitical' idea. Plato's exemplary philosophers could share their women freely with other philosophers, and would breed only with partners selected for them by the state's eugenic experts. Brothels were maintained in Athens for the benefit of male lust, since women were inferior beings. Sex was of little significance for Plato, because it was of the body. What mattered was 'wisdom', for this was the province of the soul both here and in eternity.

It is no surprise, therefore, that the nature and structure of the human person promoted by the ancient Hebrews was in clear opposition, over the centuries, to prevailing dualisms which it confronted: first, that exhibited in the culture they met when they entered what is now Israel/Palestine; then later on, the culture of the Babylonians with whom they were forced to mingle in the distressing years when they were in enforced exile.

Moses was only the first of a succession of deeply religious thinkers, some of whom we in our day entitle simply by such letters as J,E,D and P (titles given to the likely strands of authorship found in the Pentateuch). These men were followed by prophets most of whose names we know. The genius of Moses was to produce a complete theology that is based upon a wholly unitary view of reality. For the Hebrews, God is one, creation is one, and God is love.

Platonism exercised huge power in Europe for fully 1600 years. While there were other Greek thinkers, like Thucidides and Aristotle, who were less dualistic in their approach, it is Plato's thought which has been most influential. And in our own age, it is dualism which appears again in 'New Age' thought. Dualistic philosophies always lay their emphasis on our human ability to seize upon the things of the spirit and so to ignore or down-play the things of matter or of the body. Thus they neglect or even demean the person of Christ; they may recognise him to be a figure of history, and an important one at that, but ultimately he is for them a human being like us all. And so, in this view Christ merely illustrates human values, he does not define them or transform them.

For example, 'New Age' thought might take very seriously the idea that human beings are made in the image of God. Therefore, so the argument would proceed, humans can rise to possess immediate fellowship with the Spirit of God in the world of the spirit. This of course leaves out any concept of the Godhead becoming incarnate in human flesh. And incarnation is precisely what Hebraic thinking leads up to, as the rest of this book will illustrate.

An attempt is thus being made to show a generation living two centuries after Christ how the Hebrew strand in our heritage has supplied us with the means of understanding who the founder of Christianity, Jesus of Nazareth, really is. And in turn to grasp the centrality of this Jesus Christ, the incarnate one, for a knowledge of the Father and an experience of the Holy Spirit. It is often claimed that the doctrine of the Trinity is not contained in the Bible. It might be true to say that it is not spelled out in the Bible - but the doctrine is certainly implied. And in turn, the triune God sheds light on the Bible and on all of human life.

Chapter One

THE HEBREW MIND

In order to understand the Old Testament, we need to know something about how the Hebrew mind works, and about how words are used in Hebrew.

The whole issue can be best understood when we inquire into how the ancient Hebrews interpreted their own makeup as persons. Only thereafter shall we be able to discover how they thought of their relationship to others, to their environment, and finally to God.

In Genesis 2, God breathed on the man formed from dust, and it became a living creature. The being is in the life, and this life or power reaches beyond the contours of the physical body. In the right context, it is extended by words, so that when Isaac has extended his blessing to Jacob he cannot take it back again, even when Esau begs him to. Likewise, power can be extended beyond the individual in the utterance of a curse.

The same kind of power, the extension of the life of the individual, attaches to the name - so that using an important name in blessing enhances the blessing. Again, a servant can use the name of his master (as happened to procure a wife for Isaac). Likewise, the life of an individual is extended, first outwards in the extended family or household, and then down the generations through descendants. This whole family is the extended personality of the man (or woman, in some cases) at the head.

Franz Boaz has pointed out in *The History of Anthropology* (1904) that "language is intimately connected with 'ethnic psychology'". There are Polynesian languages that have no words for 'father' or 'mother'. The modern Hungarian language is without genders, it possesses only one little, single syllable word that has to do for our 'he', 'she', or 'it'. Chinese characters are largely symbols of psychological expressions of thought. We should therefore not be surprised to find in Biblical Hebrew, some of it from three thousand years ago (!) words and expressions that are very often untranslatable literally into modern English.

Take, for example, the well known line of the psalmist, "This is the day that the Lord has made, let us rejoice and be glad in it". This exhortation could equally well be translated, "Let us rejoice and be glad in him".

Consider now two simple words: 'good' and 'word', translated with difficulty and in a variety of ways in modern versions.

1 **The term 'good'** occurs in the well known story of the baby Moses of Exodus 2. The Hebrew runs, "The baby was *tob*". What does that word mean? Did it mean that Moses was a healthy child? Was he a good-looking baby, or was he 'goodly' (KJV), or 'fine' (RSV, NAB, GNB), or even 'morally good'? None of these English words is what the author of Exodus wants us to know about this baby. (Surely all mothers believe that their new-born baby is lovely!) We read on, however, in that same chapter to discover how God used the drastic plans of the baby's parents as they hoped to save their little one from the wrath of Pharaoh. Both parents were Levites, that is to say, good folk, believers in a God who has a plan for each human life. So, in a real act of faith they handed their baby into God's care, by committing him to float away down the Nile in a basket of reeds.

Moreover, their faith was truly justified. Baby Moses was indeed good for God's plan for all Israel. On the one hand, he was indeed a 'goodly' child, he lived to a ripe old age, so that *tob* points to his healthy appearance. On the other hand God saw him not simply in a human way, but as a key element in his plan for the redemption of the world. So the little word *tob* is employed by the author of Exodus as we might describe a coin. *Tob* is one small word, but, like a coin, it has two sides, each of which in some sense, interprets the other.

This kind of illustration is vital to a proper understanding of what the Old Testament, and indeed what the whole Christian faith, is about. Jesus made exactly this point when his enemies tried to trap him with a question about paying taxes. Jesus replied, "Show me a coin" (the Roman denarius). Any coin has two faces. Literally, the denarius would have on one side the face of the current Emperor of the Roman Empire. But on the other side it would have an indication of its value: and when cast into the offering box at the door of the temple it served to forward God's saving plan for the redemption of the world.

Jesus used this illustration of one coin, two sides, to answer his critics. On the one side, the coin showed the authority of the Roman emperor. But on the other, its value raised deeper questions - about the ultimate purpose of life, money, taxes. Hence his reply: "Give to Caesar what belongs to Caesar, and to God what belongs to God". On the relationship of God and Caesar hangs not only a question about taxes, but a question about life and about theology.

We shall use this illustration of the coin frequently to help us understand how human and divine relate in the unity of God's creative and redemptive purpose for the world - neither dualism, nor monism, but relationship prefigured in the Old Testament, and revealed fully in the incarnation of Christ.

Genesis 1:31 illustrates further the two-way meaning of *tob*. The creation, we read, God saw to be good, very good. Now, was it the goodness of a perfect machine, all 'wheels within wheels', comprising an unspeakably complex universe with everything working in perfect harmony - yes, it could mean just that, from our human and scientifically minded view of the cosmos. But *tob* here, from God's point of view must also mean "good for the whole plan of God's redemptive purpose which ensues from here on." Accordingly God can rest on the seventh 'day', deeply satisfied that his plan of redemption will ultimately be complete. There are some Hebrew language terms that cannot be understood unless they are seen to possess in themselves a dual meaning.

It is no accident that God revealed himself in a particular language and a particular culture. The time would come when God took on human being definitively, in Jesus of Nazareth. Now a metaphor like the two sided coin may help Gentiles to understand the incarnation - but the concept of incarnation, as we shall see, is more than metaphor, it is at the heart of how God reveals himself.

2 The term 'word' is the second basic term - in Hebrew, the root *d-b-r*. Written thus it occurs as both a verb and as a noun, with vowels to suit as the case may be. As a noun it may mean 'word', and as a verb it may mean 'say', while the verb and the noun may occur together: "He said, *d-b-r*, a word, *d-b-r*, to me."

We can best grasp the unique use of this root if we discover how it occurs with God as subject, and to do so we may imagine a comic strip in a newspaper arranged in a succession of frames. This is the second basic illustration which helps us to grasp the relation of God to the world, and understand why dualism is false.

The first frame portrays God like a human figure, with his heart exposed to view. This is because the ancient Semite spoke from his heart, where we would say 'mind', believing it to be the organ that produced all his thoughts, reasonings and emotions. The second frame shows movement, and we are given to see the thought issuing from the mouth in the form of a spoken word. The third frame now depicts the word moving from the mouth like an arrow which then strikes the ear of another figure, the one who is being addressed by the speaker. Fourth, we see the word, still in the shape of an arrow, entering, let us say, the heart of the other person through his ear and lodging in his inner being. But that is not all. The final frame shows us the second person now in action in obedience to the word that the first has uttered.

This word of God is the extension of his person and therefore his power. It does things. What his word says, God does.

In the so-called 'historical' books of the Old Testament we meet with the two Books of Chronicles, meaning 'historical records'; yet their title in Hebrew is: "The words of the days of...". We then have to translate this by: "The Acts of the period of...". But who was it who said the words in the first place so that, when uttered, they became historical events? We are led to ask this question when we remember that a word is not an entity in itself, but is to be grasped as a living part of the speaker since it has issued from the living heart of a living person. Being itself alive, it can thereupon 'do' what its sender can expect it to do. She may say: "John, shut the door", whereupon John acts and shuts the door. The Hebrew title of these books of Chronicles is therefore like our two-sided coin, it has a dual meaning. These books are indeed historical narrative about human activities; at the same time they reveal the effect in history of the Word spoken by God.

A certain centurion said to Jesus, "I also am a man under authority, with soldiers under me; and I say to one, 'Go' and he goes..., 'Do this', and he does it." The soldier would not have acted at all but would have just remained standing had not his commanding officer first said the word "Go". This understanding therefore of the vitality of the word uttered by a human person has great bearing for the Hebrew mind when it refers to God. God creates, we are told, by his word. So the realm of nature is not just a vast automatic machine, with an infinite number of wheels within wheels, as a scientifically minded human observer might declare; 'fact' is not separated from 'value', rather, nature itself is *tob*, good, not simply in itself but also in its purpose; nature has heard a Voice saying, "Be fruitful and multiply":

And in turn, the events of nature can illustrate the purpose of God among human beings:

> For as the rain and the snow come down from heaven,
> and do not return there until they have watered the earth,
> making it bring forth and sprout,
> giving seed to the sower and bread to the eater,
> so shall My Word be that goes out from my mouth;
> it shall not return to me empty,
> but it shall accomplish that which I purpose,
> and succeed in the thing for which I sent it.
>   (Isaiah 55:10-11)

Many other cases exist where terms may not be merely calling a spade a spade but are actually carrying within them a dual meaning and so producing a theological intent.

God led Moses to the 'backside' of the desert, meaning first a particular geographical wilderness; but second, it was the 'backside' of creation - a figure for the chaos of non-being, referred to at Genesis 1:2, where there was no meaning to events. Yet it was there that God addressed Moses in the Burning Bush (Exodus 3:1)!

When Jehoshaphat 'appointed singers', the verb used includes the result of his action, for the singers then sang (2 Chronicles 20:21). Similarly, a reference to the 'hand' of the Lord means not just a limb of his 'body', but includes what he does with it, for by lifting his hand he exerts his power. For example, at Numbers 11:23 we read: "The Lord himself said to Moses, 'Is the Lord's hand (that is, power) limited?' Now you shall see whether my word shall come true for you or not."

The words of Jesus in the Gospels are given to us in Greek. Originally they would be in Hebrew or Aramaic. So, in Matthew 5 we have the well known saying, "Blessed are the poor in spirit." In Luke's Gospel, we have "Blessed are you poor." In his sermon, however, on both occasions Jesus would have used only the one little word *dal*. *Dal* covers both the physical and the spiritual. It can mean to go slowly, to be reduced to poverty, but (on the back of the coin!) it can also mean to be depressed mentally.

The Old Testament writers, with this propensity for 'double-talk' in their make-up, often resorted to the use of puns - perhaps with tongue in cheek! One day, the prophet Amos was gazing round him in Jerusalem's market when his eye fell upon a basket of summer-fruit (Amos 8:1-2). These last two words in the English are in Hebrew the one word *qayts*. Immediately the pun came into his mind and he pronounced it to himself as *qets*, where now it means 'end'. His pun then became the basis for a sermon he preached. The summer fruit were over-ripe and gone bad: so had the people of Israel. "The end", says God, "has come upon my people Israel". And it did, not so long after.

In Jeremiah 1.11-12 the prophet uses the Hebrew consonants *sh-k-d* in two ways, one meaning 'almond tree' the other 'on the watch'. It is important to know Hebrew well enough to grasp the *double entendre*. There is the well known story of the American evangelist preaching from his soap-box at a street corner in Cairo, Egypt. The Arabic language is a relative of Hebrew, and shares with it the same consonants that mean the word 'dog'. This is the word *kalb*. But the word for 'heart', *qalb*, sounds to the untrained ear just like the other word. Much to the amusement of his Muslim audience, our evangelist was calling upon those good Egyptians to give their dog to Jesus.

A related point: the same word in biblical times can have a very different meaning from its use in modern Western culture. A dog, for example, is a dog in any language. But the Syrophoenician woman whom Jesus encountered (Mark 7:27-28) was speaking, not of a household pet as we envisage in our culture, but of a vicious, half-starved, despised animal of the streets.

Wind and spirit are the same word in Hebrew. How then do we translate Genesis 1:2? "A wind from God swept over the face of the waters", or "A spirit from God swept....". Evidently the physical is interpreted by the spiritual and vice versa - one coin, two sides. Jesus made use of this two-sided word when he talked with Nicodemus saying "The wind (spirit) flows where it (he, she?) chooses" (John 3:1-8).

Yashar, 'upright', describes a vertical pillar of the temple, but it is also used to describe a person who is morally upright, as in English.

Again, one and one do not always make two. "God separated the light from the darkness. God called the light Day, and the darkness he called Night" - yet he called them, both together, one day! (Genesis 1:4-5).

"O God, I have looked upon you in the sanctuary beholding your power and glory" (Psalm 63:2). How could that be? Because in seeing the physical one sees God, one glimpses the spiritual with which it is one. Naturally then there is no word for supernatural in the Old Testament. That idea belongs to pluralist thinking, not to a theology of oneness. In the Old Testament there is only the physical world and God who created it.

The meaning of one 'side' of a speech or an action can convey the meaning of the 'whole' and transfer that whole to another object or person. We have: "The heart of the people melted and became water" (Joshua 7:5), not, let us note, "became like water" but "became water" - the picture is of the heart of the people together as one corporate entity. In the same way, a poet can say, "The moon shall be turned into blood" (Joel 2:31; Hebrews 3:4; quoted at Acts 2:20). We might call this a case of the pregnant thinking of the Hebrew mind; but such thinking can become the medium of profound theological significance when we find the command, "Be sure that you do not eat the blood; for the blood is the life" (Leviticus 17:14).

So now, in the light of all the above usages, we may turn to the Hebraic belief in the composition of the human person that we find described in the second creation story (Genesis 2). This chapter is from the hand of the anonymous theologian to whom scholars give the title of 'J', for two reasons. First, he knows God as *Jahweh* (or *Yahweh*), whereas in chapter one God is known as *Elohim*, the title used mostly by the author(s) of 'P' in the Pentateuch; these were highly intellectual and theologically minded priests. The second reason is that it was probably made in Jerusalem. Chapter one offers us the creation of humankind in conceptual terms, chapter two, from the hand of J, uses descriptive narrative. Incidentally this is the form that prevails with both the prophets and much of the teaching of Jesus.

The 'story' goes how the LORD God (the capital letters in English used in LORD refer to the Hebrew title Yahweh) "formed man from the dust of the ground, and breathed into his nostrils the breath of life (Genesis 2:7), and the man became a living being." 'The man' employs the Hebrew generic article as does P at Genesis 1:27. There God had created *ha-adam*, humankind, not Adam - both male and female as one by the utterance of the Word: "Then God said..." and humanity became. J gives us the picture of God's action until we see the new thing originating from the tangible breath of God, which, of course, conveys the invisible Word with its creative power.

'A living being' requires a new word. It is 'a living *nephesh*', living, because the living God has spoken what is his living Word - effectively. As we have quoted before, "So shall my word be that goes out from my mouth; it shall not return to me empty but it shall accomplish that which I purpose and succeed in the thing for which I sent it" (Isaiah 55:11). "By the word of the Lord the heavens were made, and all their host by the breath of his mouth" (Psalm 33:6). So too here, God breathed his breath into what is 'flesh', *basar*, the dust of the ground, and thereby created humanity (both sexes) - in his own image (so P), as a living being, *nephesh*, (so J).

This is a clear picture of human beings as one entity. In contrast with the dualistic world of the period, there is no suggestion that we 'have' a soul that merely lodges in our bodies; we 'are' body and soul - one living *nephesh* in the image of the one living God.

So far is the language of our culture today from that of Genesis that we possess no word in English that can render *nephesh*. Dualistic philosophies and theologies have kept on surfacing throughout the whole history of the Christian church. Emphasis was so often placed upon the salvation of the soul that even the theology of orthodoxy could ignore the significance of the body. Doctors were known to search within the cadaver they were dissecting for what they hoped to find as the seat of the soul, now departed. And, unfortunately, sections of the Christian church, even now, pay scant attention to the call of the prophet Micah (6:8) to put justice for the social claims of the world's poor before any thought of our own personal and private hopes and claims to "walk humbly with our God". Too often Christians have focused upon saving 'souls', since souls are immortal, but not on feeding the hungry, since hunger is of the flesh that perishes.

Old Testament Hebrew uses the one word *nephesh* for the person of a man or a woman. That is to say, it ignores any differences it may recognise do actually exist between male and female. The Hebrew pronoun *hu* covers both genders. It may be rendered 'he' if a male person is specifically in question, but most often, in its unitary nature, it means both 'he' and 'she'. Of course, English has no word for this unitary Hebrew pronoun. Other modern languages do have, if not pronouns then nouns. The German language puts brothers and sisters into one word (*geschwistern*). German has 'felt' the reality of the Hebraic pattern of thought. The English equivalent of that word 'brethren' does not please those brought up in English culture who suppose that sisters are not included in that term! Again the word *ben* ('son', 'son of') with its plural *banim, bene*, can and does mean both young males and children of both sexes as one whole, eg. *bene Yisrael* we render 'Children of Israel'. Paul clinched the matter later on as a true Hebrew of the Hebrews by declaring that "In Christ there is neither male nor female" (Galatians 3:28). Feminist theologians in our day might do well to look to see if they are not perhaps captives of their own pluralist English culture, and therefore unable to grasp the biblical theology of the Incarnation.

Again it is necessary for us to see what the Hebrew actually says. God does not breathe his Spirit *ruah* into an existing human being. That would lead to a false theology. *Ruah* is the gift of God which then makes the man a *nephesh*, and not just *basar*, body. *Ruah* takes the form of muscular strength in Samson, of dexterity in those who built the Tabernacle, of prophecy in the case of Micah. In his case the *ruah* enabled each part of the *basar*, the flesh, whether the ear, hand, eye, bowels, to act on behalf of the whole *nephesh*. This oneness is indicated when we see how the part could speak for the whole, as in Psalm 63:1 which reads: "O God, you are my God, my *nephesh* thirsts for you, my *basar* faints for you." Psalm 26:2 says: "Prove me, O LORD, and try me; test my heart (*leb*) and mind (really 'kidneys', *kilyoth*)". So again at Proverbs 23:16 "My kidneys (NRSV 'soul'!) will rejoice when you speak what is right". Psalm 51:8 (Hebrew v10) runs, "Let the bones that you have crushed rejoice."

A part of the body acting for the whole is noticeable in expressions that are conveyed pictorially, such as, "Incline your ear" (Psalm 86:1), or "All my people shall order themselves according to your mouth" (NRSV, "as you command", Genesis 41:40). David said to Ahimelech, "The King's *dabar* (word? business?) required haste" (1 Samuel 21:8).

Clearly since flesh and spirit may perform identical functions, and since the blood is the life, the Hebrew thinking conceived of the human personality as a unity of consciousness, though indeed a unity in diversity. A human *nephesh* was not a mere human 'union' of flesh and spirit. Consequently Hebrew thought faced an insoluble problem when a whole *nephesh* was placed in the grave! For obviously it was the *basar*, the fleshly element of a person that perished under the soil. So adamant were our scholarly Old Testament thinkers in this matter that they were unable to entertain any hopes for a life beyond death. They were quite unlike the dualistic masses of the nations all around them who almost all believed that the soul was a separate entity, so that when the body died the soul could then escape and enter the life beyond.

The Hebrews' fellow citizens and neighbours, the Canaanites, mostly held the view that there was an underworld to which dead 'souls' descended; they knew it as Sheol. Untheologically minded Israelites were often attracted to believe in this empty, hollow place, as the name Sheol may have meant in the beginning, though true believers did not succumb to this view. They rejected even a belief in ghosts and "things that go bump in the night" for the same reason. In consequence his contemporaries reckoned King Saul was sinning even to suppose that he could talk to the ghost of Samuel (1 Samuel 28:8ff.).

We shall keep this in mind later when we discover how the New Testament writers took over and transformed the old Hebraic view of death, and this they were able to do because they took over also the Hebraic concept of the human personality, along with the language that described it.

Another important linguistic use by many present-day languages is one which came naturally to the ancient Hebrews. This was to describe a whole family, tribe or even nation as one *nephesh*. Through the Prophets God can address all Israel as 'she' when emphasis was laid upon the capital city of Jerusalem. A city was feminine, Jerusalem was often called Zion, a poetic name, so the feminine Zion could be used of all Israel as one. The same applied to any nation. As one people, one *nephesh*, Babylon, Egypt, Tyre were each one 'she'. Jesus even used the idiom, when he cried, "O Jerusalem, Jerusalem ... as a hen (feminine) gathers her chickens under her wings" (Matthew 23:37).

Since all Israel, in the early days, saw herself as one *nephesh* she could say to Moab on her journey from Sinai to the Promised land: "Let me pass through thy land". In consequence of this way of understanding the nature of community it is not surprising to find Second Isaiah, centuries later, declaring to the scattered Israelite individuals in the chaotic society in which the exiled Hebrews were perforce wearily spending their days - and years!: "Here is my servant, whom I uphold, my chosen, in whom my soul (*nephesh* - so God is a *nephesh* also!) delights" (Isaiah 42:1). Would the prophet have been able thus to interpret the mind of God as he did, had the ordinary Israelites not learned to picture themselves as a psychic unit?

Moreover we find that the head of the whole body of this psychic unit, in this case the king, held a unique psychical relationship to the whole people. When the destruction of Jerusalem finally took place, whose 'end' Amos had declared was inevitable, mourning for his dead king a poet could say, "The LORD's anointed, the breath of our life, was taken in their pits - the one of whom we said: 'Under his shadow we shall live among the nations'" (Lamentations 4:20). As the Second Isaiah pursues his argument in Isaiah 40-55 we find him speaking of all Israel as one *nephesh*, as being God's chosen servant, but at the same time described as if that servant were epitomised in the *nephesh* of only one individual. Exodus carries the same meaning, when God describes Moses as his 'first-born son' (Exodus 4:22).

We proceed now to discover in chapter two what is the nature of God. We have first looked at the nature of men and women, and their ways of thought, as the Hebrews conceived them. This is important for biblical theology, as God has chosen to reveal himself at a human level - and that implies creating in Hebrew language and thought an adequate unitary way of thinking about people. In the Hebrew picture of human beings we find a revelation from God of human nature. In many ways this is just as important as the revelation in the Bible of the true nature of God.

In the Bible, the knowledge of God and of human being go together. Since God has chosen to reveal himself through human beings, it is important to understand what human being is if we are to understand God - and vice versa.

Chapter Two

THE BEING OF GOD

How did people in Old Testament times face the mystery of the divine? Were the early Hebrews really monotheists, or were they, like their neighbours around them, believers in many gods and goddesses, or 'powers', or other pluralistic forms of the divine?

It may well have been so before the trained mind and profound faith of Moses were applied to this basic issue. There may well have been any number of divine beings in the ancient Hebrew pantheon, as there was even for such intellectual peoples as the ancient Greeks. In fact, to use the Old Testament term, there may well have been 'hosts' of divine beings beyond human reach. But let us note, the English word 'host' translates the Hebrew term 'army', and that puts a different complexion upon what we suppose the early Hebrews believed. For, from Moses onwards the supreme God, *El*, was in reality 'Lord of Hosts', the one and only Lord of everything - which is why the opening verse of the Bible can equally well be translated, "In the beginning God created the heavens and the earth", or as "....... created the universe". The 'heavens' are literally higher than us, but they are still part of space and time.

In his strongly worded testimony to Joshua his successor, as we have it in Deuteronomy 32:1-43 (the so-called *Song of Moses*), the great leader accuses his people of polytheistic activities:

> They sacrificed to demons, not God,
> to deities they had never known,
> to new ones recently arrived,
> whom your ancestors had not feared. (v.17)

But then he adds two lines that refer to the basic faith that Moses had taught them, pointing to the reality that it was actually the living God as their Creator-Father (v.40) who had chosen them and birthed them:

> You were unmindful of the Rock that bore you;
> You forgot the God who gave you birth. (v.18)

As Moses pointed out, their very existence depended upon God. He had created Israel as his people. The nations around them had done the reverse, they had all created their gods in their own image. We hear of these gods quarrelling, fornicating, murdering somewhere up in the sky, simply because their worshippers quarrelled, fornicated, murdered somewhere below on earth. To use a modern phrase, Zeus, the king of the gods on Mount Olympus "leaped from one bed to another of his female court". Instead the story of Israel began with grace, by an act of God, the Rock of Ages, the eternal, unchangeable, 'alpha and omega', the beginning and the end. Here is how it is described:

> The LORD brought us up out of the land of Egypt, out of the house of bondage.

This statement dealt with fact. Their 'birth' was not of their own doing. God had taken the initiative and had acted first in grace, as Moses explained it, and had made a covenant with his people, wicked as they were; and this strangely different God had put these words in Moses' mouth:

> Thus you shall say to the house of Jacob, and tell the Israelites: "You have seen what I did to the Egyptians, and how I bore you on eagles' wings and brought you to myself. Now therefore, if you obey my voice and keep my covenant, you shall be my treasured possession out of all the peoples. Indeed, the whole earth is mine, but you shall be for me a priestly kingdom and a holy nation. These are the words that you shall speak to the Israelites." (Exodus 19:4-6)

There was a potency in the utterance of the Word, as Second Isaiah, far away, centuries later, and sharing in the horrors of the exile in Babylon, could believe and interpret at two points:

(1) "While I was stretching out the heavens and laying the foundations of the earth, I was saying to Zion, 'You are my people'" (Isaiah 51:16); and

(2) "It is too light a thing that you should be my servant to raise up the tribes of Jacob (despondent in exile) and to restore the survivors of Israel; I will give you as a light to the nations, that my salvation may reach to the end of the earth" (Isaiah 49:6).

That is what it meant to be a priestly kingdom. So God is one, God is Saviour, and God is Love, and God works through an 'incarnational' relationship with his one chosen servant on earth. He did so through a Word spoken with effect, with results in history; in and through a new form of covenantal relationship, as the "Word became flesh".

What then does the word 'one' mean? Is it simply a 'mathematical unit', as the English could be understood? Ever since the year 1611 the English speaking public have known the King James Version rendering as "The Lord our God is one LORD". (See *The Lord is One*, Expository Times, December, 1966, for a fuller discussion of the two words).

Some modern versions vary from this. The New English Bible says, "The LORD is our God, one LORD". The Good News Bible offers three alternative renderings: "The LORD - and the LORD alone - is our God"; "The LORD our God is the only God"; "The LORD our God is one". The Revised Standard Version offers us four suggestions, all of them emphasising that God is one and alone. The New Revised Standard Version accepts these four, and then adds still another. But all these attempts to render the Hebrew word for 'one', that occurs here in the original Hebrew, seem to be concerned to tell us that the LORD our God is unique, the one and only God there is or can be.

Now the Hebrew language does possess a word for 'one' in this sense, *yahid*. It could amply supply us with the information that God is unique. A strong example of the use of *yahid* occurs at Genesis 22:2,16: "Take your son, your only son Isaac...". But *yahid* is not used here. It is *ehad* that appears at Deuteronomy 6:4 and this term occurs some 160 times in the Hebrew Old Testament. This word can and does mean 'one' in the mathematical sense, as in the English jingle, "One is one and all alone..."; but that reality can also be expressed by the root *b-d-d* ('separate off' where at Psalm 4:8, we read, "For you alone, O LORD, make me to lie down *in safety*").

But when we hear the voice of Ezekiel at 11:19 declaring for God: "I will give them one heart", the one new heart in which the many will share, we begin to wonder if there is not more to *ehad* than uniqueness. "We will live among you and become one people" (Genesis 34:16), even though the one people is comprised of many individuals. "So all the men of Israel gathered against the city, united as one" (Judges 20:11).

We can take another step. The ideas of singular and plural may occur together as one phrase, eg. "Join (the sticks) together into one, *ehad*, stick" (Ezekiel 37:17), clearly because the two together are one in function. But most importantly we can note the well known words: "Therefore a man leaves his father and his mother and clings to his wife, and they become one flesh": again, one in function (Genesis 2:24). That is to say their oneness has been formed from two ordinary 'ones' to be a new unit in God's plan for the redemption of all things.

So the word *ehad* appears to have two meanings, again like two sides of a coin. Consequently if we seek carefully what the word *ehad* meant for those who used it in the Old Testament times, this will shed light on what it means to believe in one God today.

The unique God of Israel became known to his people as one, all-comprehensive, united, complete and whole *nephesh*. It would seem that Paul, in trying to 'expound God' to non-Hebraic congregations employed the Greek term *pleroma* ('fullness' in the NRSV) as the equivalent of the wholeness, the completeness that the Hebrew word *ehad* conveyed in that language (Ephesians 2:15-16; 3:19; cf Jeremiah 23:24). Contrary-wise, therefore, God must exclude from his nature, from his wholeness, all other gods in both heaven and earth.

One of the last and final declarations of any voice in the Old Testament is made by the prophet scholars call Second Zechariah (Zech 14:9): "And the LORD will become king over all the earth; on that day the LORD will be one, and his name one, *ehad*." Whereas in later centuries Mohammed can declare in the Qoran: "There is no god but God", thereby expressing what the Hebrew would have meant by *yahid*, he was manifesting a different form of monotheism from that found in Deuteronomy 6:4.

The significance of the word *ehad* for one is a key stage in the process that leads finally to an understanding of the Incarnation of Christ and of Christianity as a faith, in contrast to Islam.

The root Semitic term for the Divine Being, *El*, is found, as we have noted, in the Old Testament, especially in poetic passages. Learning from its use in other cultures, we discover it probably meant "the Mighty One". From that same root, *Eloah*, another singular title, is the most used word for God in the book of Job. But scholars virtually agree that 'Job' is the product of the particular Wisdom that had its seat, not in Judah, but somewhere east of Jordan where the caravans from the different cultures of Persia and Arabia mixed and met with scholars from the traditional Holy Land. And of course the Arabic *Allah* is virtually the same as *Eloah*.

We are left with two titles for Israel's God, each of them occurring, not hundreds, but indeed thousands of times in the Hebrew Bible, in fact quite frequently bound together, as if each interpreted the other, viz as LORD GOD. LORD is the singular title *Yahweh*, while GOD, *Elohim* is a plural. Now they may each have originated separately in Israel's early story, *Yahweh* possibly in Judah's traditions, and *Elohim* possibly in northern Israel; yet when later the traditions were collated in the editing process, it is evident that in the text of the Old Testament that has come down to us, each meant the same as the other. The singular *Yahweh* was evidently the name of the God of the Covenant (Exodus 19:5; 24:8), while *Elohim* became equally the only name possible for the God of creation (Genesis 1:1).

There have been scholars who have suggested this plural word for God (-*im* is the plural masculine suffix) was a way of expressing magnitude, but on the basis of the Hebrew way of thinking we can recognise that this was how Old Testament theologians found it suitable to express God's oneness and diversity at the same time. Consequently they applied a singular verb to the plural noun as subject, "And *Elohim* said..." (singular).

As a plural term, *Elohim* could be described as having fellowship within himself. He seems to talk to himself when, for example, we read: "God said, let us make man in our image" (Genesis 1:27). In the Song of Moses already quoted (Deuteronomy 32:1-43), first it is Moses who challenges his people to do God's will. But suddenly, at v.20, we have God speaking to himself about Israel's disloyalty, and saying: "I will hide my face from them, I will see what their end will be."

This discovery clarifies for us how the ancient Hebrews conceived of God as one corporate personality, in modern language indeed a 'personality', not a philosophical abstraction. His personal nature is then exemplified by the use of anthropomorphic terms. God is described as using his voice, his hand, his eye, his ear. But in every case it is God's hand, God's ear that is referred to, in the sense that each 'bodily' organ is acting for the 'whole' of the Person of God, and that the 'whole' of God's Being is present in the part. Thus when God "lends an ear to my cry", my cry reaches right to God's heart.

Along with the employment of anthropomorphisms, the Old Testament uses poetic and parabolic language to portray the 'unity in diversity' of *elohim*. "No man can see God and live" declares Moses to his recalcitrant people at the foot of Mount Sinai, owing to the reality that God is all-holy and humans are inveterate sinners.

We read that Moses and Aaron, Nadab and Abihu, and seventy of the elders of Israel went up, "and they saw the God of Israel" (Exodus 24:9-10); yet what they saw was, as always, only "something like this or that": "Now the appearance of the glory of the LORD was like a devouring fire ..." (Exodus 24:17). In fact, in all instances where human language is employed to describe the glory of God interpretation is made pictorially of this corporate unity-in-diversity of Israel's God. Contrast the Septuagint, the Greek translation of the Old Testament, produced only after the whole corpus was virtually complete, and in the cultural atmosphere of the Hellenistic world (actually in Alexandria in Egypt). That version does not appreciate the daring language of anthropomorphism and in consequence often actually alters the text.

"The heavens declare the glory of God" (Psalm 19:1) sings the Psalmist. Ezekiel the prophet, immured in far-away Babylon in the years of exile, had a profound experience of being brought back into the Jerusalem of his youth, the "city of *Yahweh*" itself. He reports: "And there, the glory of the God of Israel was coming from the east; the sound was like the sound of many waters; and the earth shone with his glory" (Ezekiel 43:2). "Enter into the rock, and hide in the dust from the terror of the LORD, and from the glory of his majesty", warns the prophet Isaiah (Isaiah 2:10), "and the LORD alone will be exalted in that day" (v.11). Indeed, the LORD alone, yet 'personally' represented by his glory through which he reveals the 'wholeness' of his Being to the eyes of sinners. In fact, the glory of God is sometimes actually pictured as the 'living' garment of the Holy God.

The Hebrew term *kabod* may express what seems to us to have widely different meanings. In the human story of Jacob we find that his 'wealth' was his 'glory' (Genesis 3:11). He 'wore' his wealth for all to see. Sometimes a man's glory was defined as the 'honour' due to him for being successful in life, and this result he 'wore' in the 'dignity' (*kabod*) he now possessed in the eyes of his neighbours. At Numbers 24:11 we read: "I will reward you richly", rendered in the NRSV as "I will glorify you gloriously", using the root of *kabod*.

So, in the area of anthropomorphism we can return to what Israel has to say about the glory of God. God may actually transfer his glory (still the term *kabod*), not his essential Being, of course, to his covenant people. Psalm 89:15 runs: "Happy are the people who know the festal shout, who walk, O LORD, in the light of your Face... for you are the glory of their strength". Nor is God's glory a mere static quality. God is the living God (*El hai*). So he continues to reveal himself to us in his actions (cf. Luke 4:14, 7:21-23), down from 'heaven' to 'earth' below. He declared he would do so when his glory descended most overwhelmingly upon and in amongst his 'godforsaken' children of Israel when they were 'lost' in the chaotic mixture of cultures in Nebuchadnezzar's Babylon: "I bring near my deliverance, it is not far off ... I will put salvation in Zion, for Israel my glory".

This vital promise of God must obviously bear within it a powerful potential for action upon humankind. (We recall from chapter 1 how the word 'good' in the Exodus 2 description of the baby Moses must spill over into its own result and so means 'good for' God's plan of redemption.) Manoah had said to his wife, "We shall surely die, for we have seen God" (Judges 13:22). The power of the promise that she, even in her old age, would have a baby, is evidently able to break through the veil that human sin has entangled them in, in an act of total mercy and forgiveness. "Woe is me, for I am lost ... yet my eyes have seen the King, the LORD of Hosts", exclaimed the young Isaiah (6:5) when at worship in the Temple.

At 2 Chronicles 5:14, 7:2 the priests, through their ordination, had access to the Holy Place of the Temple, when even the Levites were not able to endure the manifestation of the glory of the LORD, "for the glory of the LORD (*Yahweh*, the God of the Covenant) filled the house of God (*Elohim* the Creator God of the universe and of all mankind)". And yet, here we have a new and thrilling revelation of the saving love and power of God. "May your sinful priests", prays the Psalmist (Psalm 132:16) "be clothed with salvation, with God's saving love", even as God himself is "clothed with salvation".

We are now able to see that the revelation of God is never of God in the abstract, but of God in action. He is the God (how often are we told this!) "who brought us up out of slavery in Egypt into the Promised Land". Moreover, this fact should always keep us in mind that there is no such thing as love in the abstract. "Love is not a pink smell in the room", I once heard a fine old Methodist bishop declare to a gathering of students at a youth conference. "Love is God", says the Indian mystic. No, says the Hebraist in reply, what we must declare is that "God is love", for love is known only through actions, the actions of a living Person. Love is even made visible in the giving of a cup of cold water to a thirsty man.

Another important term whose unique use is made to reveal the nature and being of God is that of the 'name'. At the human level, just as the *nephesh* possesses a body, so it also possesses a name. Yet more than 'possesses' - for the name of a man was thought to be identical with him as a person. S.A. Cooke, in his *The Old Testament, a Reinterpretation* p.106, expresses this concept neatly: "The name is both the label and the packet." Proverbs 10:7 declares that it is not the wicked who rot for their sins, but the name of the wicked. The name is so fully representative of the character that if a man's character changes, then his name must change too. A blessing could do it. A blessing is a word spoken with intent sufficient to change the recipient of the blessing. Accordingly when Abram received a blessing from God, he also received the new name of Abraham (Genesis 17:5).

God too has a name, and just as with human beings, God's name can represent its owner, and even act on its owner's behalf (see 2 Samuel 6:2; 1 Chronicles 13:6; 2 Chronicles 6:5,33). God can be invoked in worship by name, thus allowing something of himself to be revealed. At Exodus 19:3 we read that at Mount Sinai Moses went up to *Elohim* (God as Creator and Ruler over all), and heard Yahweh call to him from the mountain, revealing the name of the God of the Covenant. Here then God has two names, revealing the 'two sides of the coin' that is God the Creator, and God the Saviour.

As there had been a prelude to the giving of the law in the form of a divine speech (Exodus 19:1-5), so at 23:30 there is a postlude, again in the form of a divine speech. It runs: "I am going to send an angel (*mal'akh*, messenger) in front of you, to guard you on the way and to bring you to the place that I have prepared. Be attentive to him, and listen to his voice; do not rebel against him, for he will not pardon your transgression; for **my name** is in him".

This is a deeply theological statement. Who can forgive sins but God alone? Has this angel then usurped the place of God? Is this angel a second God for Israel to be attentive to and whose voice they were to obey? Such an idea is excluded totally from Moses' or any other

Israelite's framework of thought, for the Hebrews were not pluralistic, nor were they even dualists, as were the Canaanite peoples around them. The answer comes in the final phrase: "For My name is in him".

What name? Nowhere are we ever told, for what is human can never seize hold of the essence of the divine. To be able to do so was excluded from within the cultural *Weltanschauung* of 1300 BCE in the Sinai desert; and since God is the same yesterday, today, and will be forever, no human mind, however brilliant, is able to classify and understand the mind of God any more than any ancient, Plato, Buddha or any other philosopher could ever do.

Yet there we have it - "My name is in him", in the form of a promise of divine revelation - not of impersonal scientific knowledge of the nature of God, but of being able to 'know' God, *yada'*. To know God is not the same as to know about God. Here the English language is poor. The French language carefully offers us here two words for the one word in English - *savoir* is to know that two and two make four, while *connaître* refers to the total knowledge a married couple have of each other. So intimate is the Hebrew *yada'* that it covers the physical, psychical and spiritual experience of the true human marriage covenant. For example, because Israel in the prophet Amos' day is living in covenant with *Yahweh*, he can say to her: "You only have I known of all the families of the earth, therefore..." (Amos 3:2).

There are other ways of speaking about God which reveal his nature. For example, in knowing 'the Angel of the Covenant', who led the people through the desert, Israel becomes aware that she is coming to know God himself; this is because his name has been extended right into the heart of Israel's life and experience, even while God remains the unknown God.

Many centuries later, at Isaiah 63:8-9, the prophet of the return from exile refers to this promise of God as applying to that event as much as it did to the events of Moses' day, but emphasises that it was not the Angel who was important but what mattered was the presence of God in the Angel, the Angel being but the agent of God's activity as "their saviour in all their distress".

The Temple was the place God would choose as a dwelling for his Name (Deuteronomy 12:11). Accordingly the priests were to place before his presence ('face' in Hebrew) 'bread of the face' fresh each day; like the Name, the Face (Exodus 25:30) gave Israel a sacramental theology that has consequences to this day. Israel learned that God does not just reveal his will through these various means, the Name, the Angel, the Face, but performs his will through them by his Holy Spirit.

We are to note that the Spirit is not another God. It is always the Spirit of God that is mentioned, just as with the Face of God, the

Name of God, and the Angel of God. Similarly it is true of the Word. The Word is always of God, for it is God who speaks the Word.

All these four terms are masculine nouns. It looks as if, being such, they are agents of a masculine God. The balance, however, is maintained when we find that the feminine 'Personality', Wisdom, is described in great detail in Proverbs 1:20-21 and in chapter 8. This balance thus reminds us that God, though 'Person', is neither male nor female; for "God is Spirit and those who worship him must worship in spirit and truth" - words of Jesus himself at John 4:24. God's Person is beyond gender.

"In the beginning" - it sounds like Genesis 1:1 - "I was brought forth", like a baby girl (Proverbs 8:24); "then I was beside him like a master worker"; she knows and expresses the epitome of joy as she watches God's creative powers at work, but especially "delights in the human race". This is all anthropomorphism to a high degree, clearly seen in the employment of a very common verb: "The LORD 'created' me in the beginning of his work." *Qanah* is quite imprecise in meaning. It may translate as 'get', which in English is imprecise. 'Get' may cover such ideas as buy, steal, purloin, receive as a gift, or again it may lead to 'beget', and so, as here, 'create'.

It is fortunate that the author of this passage about Lady Wisdom chose such an imprecise term. He was not a scientist, striving to discover exactly the relationship between God and his little 'daughter'. Instead, our Hebrew theologian satisfied himself with expressing his theological stance in picture language, in poetry of power and majesty. Science, in parallel with theology, marvels at the nature and structure of what God does. The scientist seeks to unravel the mysteries of this universe, and so 'to think God's thoughts after him'.

Chapter Three

THE UNITY THAT IS TRINITY

Walter Eichrodt (*Theology of the Old Testament I,II*) consistently made the 'covenant' not only a major Old Testament theme, but the basic framework of his Old Testament theology. A few critics complained that this choice of concept was both artificial and arbitrary. Eichrodt's reply was that the focus of his work was not simply one of several possible concepts, but actually God. So too I would suggest that my demonstration of the Hebraic awareness of the relation between, for example, matter and spirit is not simply focusing on a particular concept but actually upon God alone.

Israel did not choose Yahweh to be their God, it was God who chose Israel to be his covenant partner (Exodus 19:5), and thereafter it was through this covenant relationship that God also chose to reveal himself to humankind. God 'stooped' to use as the channels of his self-revelation the language and psychology of a rabble of slaves from amongst the Semitic peoples of the Near East, a people quite uncoordinated as a developed human group at the time of their adoption. But as this nation was step by step transformed into an organised national unit, becoming eventually a kingdom amongst the kingdoms of the world, in the covenant God kept on revealing himself, first to Israel, and then to the world through Israel in ever unique and creative forms. He did so through the thought processes and imaginative concepts of this Semitic people that could express its experience of God only in terms of its own Semitic language and Semitic world view.

The forms of speech used by the early Hebrews that we have looked at were employed by "Moses and all the prophets" (Jesus' own phrase) to express realities about our human make-up as coordinated and unitary beings. Then we have noted how the Old Testament theologians found they could use these forms of speech also when referring to the LORD their God. But what we can further discover is that this Hebraic language is not confined to the Old Testament. In the centuries that followed its completion Jewish Rabbis, owing to their intense interest in the Pentateuch (the "Five Books of Moses", the *Torah*), continued to think and write about the nature and purpose of *Yahweh*, the LORD, the God of Israel in the same terms as their biblical forefathers had done. The key to their continuing to do so was that the Rabbis knew they and their people were still in this ancient covenant relationship with *Yahweh*, and so in some sense in a unitary fellowship with their unitary God.

What happened was this. When Israel went into exile in Babylonia, and later again in 70 CE under the Romans, the sacrificial worship formalised by Moses and his successors under the command and revelation of God himself, had necessarily to be abandoned. A teaching tradition started to grow around weekly synagogue worship. This tradition continued even after the Jews were expelled from the Holy Land.

Consequently, after the close of the Canon of the Old Testament at the end of the first Christian century and after the destruction of Herod's Temple in 70 CE by the Roman power, Israel found herself developing a new epicentre. She now perforce became not "The People of the Temple" but "The People of the Book", the *Torah*, the Pentateuch. In consequence the profound and earnest examination of *Torah* and the theological discussions that derived from that examination were wholly maintained, not just in the Hebrew language jointly with the developing 'sister' language of Aramaic, but also - unwittingly, so to speak - in the cultural and grammatical, psychological and pictorial manner that is true of the prophets and Wisdom writers of old. And this was because, as I have said, the Rabbis, in the years to follow, now in exile in Egypt, Babylonia and Europe, knowing themselves still to be in a unitary, covenantal relationship with God, continued to theologise in terms that the world of pluralism beyond their walls could never understand. In fact, the roots of European Gentile Anti-Semitism lie in this strange Jewish insistence that any of the possible dualistic philosophies of the nations, whether east or west, was wrong, and so being wrong, was evil. Unless we today recognise that fact, we cannot understand what the Bible describes as the wrath of God.

A vital aspect of the divine, 'The Wrath of God' has always been a difficulty, and remains a stumbling block to many today. We tend of course to read our meanings back into the psychology of God, instead of understanding the meaning of 'God is angry' from the context. When God says, "I have become your enemy", it means that God is hostile to us in our sins, not that he is hostile in himself.

The answer goes right back to the revelatory words of Moses in Deuteronomy 32. In that chapter, known as "The Song of Moses", we possess in one whole and complete 'sermon' in verse the 'last testimony' of Moses to Joshua who was to be his successor. In it Moses shows what the wrath of God is, and why God had to reveal it to his own chosen people as 'one side of the unitary coin' that represents the nature of God - the other side being God's redeeming love. He revealed that the two are one. It has only been Hebraic thought that has given a sinful world this ultimate answer. (This is expanded in *The Song of Moses*, commentary on Deuteronomy 32:19-35.)

There is a title for Yahweh found in the Old Testament text and in post-biblical Hebrew: *Shaddai*. Its origin and meaning however have never found complete agreement. Modern versions of the Bible simply translate it by the word "Almighty", though no one can be sure that such is correct. Some think that *Shaddai* is not a Hebrew title at all, but is actually Babylonian in origin. Some have suggested that it is a compound term where we find a coupling of the single Hebrew letter *shin* ('sh' in English) with *di*, meaning "of me". Then what we are left with is *el-shadai*, "The God who is mine". Again, we possess remnants, found in quotations in other works, in actually three different translations into Greek of the Hebrew Bible, made respectively by persons called Aquila, Symmachus and Theodotion. Some suggest today that Aquila could be the person of that name mentioned at Acts 18:2. What remains of his text (well-known in the early Christian centuries) reveals that he did not appreciate the sometimes rather free translation of the 'official' Septuagint version. So his own translation was ultra-literal in its choice of terms and is made in almost Hebraised Greek. But his chosen wording in this case reveals that he was trying hard to give God's chosen people language as close to the literal meaning of a title like *Shaddai* as the scholarship of his day was able to accept. What he was seeking to do was to express in Greek that the 'personal' *Elohim* was to be pictured as no remote and far-off God, but as the God of personal relations and real presence within Israel's life.

We recall how, in Old Testament usage, God as Creator could also be named Father, and Israel be called his Son (Exodus 4:22; Deuteronomy 32:6). In fact, another Greek translation of the Semitic *Shaddai* is *hikanos*, which means 'sufficient' - sufficient for us poor humans to grasp the miracle of those 'personal relations' that render human existence a joyous and blessed experience. Or, were those translators daring to suggest that the very nature of the Divine was sufficient to himself, only because he had entered into a 'personal' relationship with his covenant people? Or again, that God was actually complete and whole even though he had spilled out the love which was of himself upon his creature man? Of course, these are only speculative thoughts, but they could have entered only those minds which conceived of God as one whole, *ehad*, and not just *yahid*, unique and lonely.

In his *The Essence of Judaism*, a standard work on Judaism, Leo Baeck says on p.63:

> It is foreign to the prophets to deduce logically, from the interconnectedness and cohesion of nature, the existence of a first cause. But the Divine unity becomes unshakeably certain to them by the inward experience that there is only one justice, only one holiness. God is the one God because he is the Holy One. The conviction of the unity of God thus has its roots in the religious consciousness.

This means that Baeck is not using the term 'unity' to mean a mathematical 'one', but is declaring what we have already noted, that

(1) since man is not a mere male, but is *ha-adam*, humankind composed of both sexes, and

(2) man is a union of flesh and spirit in his *nephesh*, then his *nephesh* is consequently a parable of the *nephesh* of God.

This belief, or, if you like, awareness of the relationship between God and humans, comes to mind when we remember that the human *nephesh* is not complete in itself, but is in reality a 'whole person' only when it is in full and fruitful relations with the *nepheshes* of others. In other words we are meant to be social beings. If that needful social relationship breaks down then it means that we are not perfectly good, but sinners. But, since the 'whole' God *ha-elohim* is holy and therefore perfectly good, he may extend his *nephesh* to his chosen and covenant people in order to empower them through his loving concern for them, to enter into true and creative relations with others in their turn. And the whole movement - from God to covenant race, and then from covenant race to all humankind - is one whole activity bound together as one by means of the initial act of grace in creation (see Isaiah 49:6). This act is God-given, not humanly achieved.

The Contemporary English Version has it right when it translates the original Hebrew as: "You must take my saving power to everyone on earth" - not send it, as a spoken or written message, but be it in the flesh. The messenger must become the message because only then does he exhibit in the wholeness of his being what God's saving power actually is and does. That is to say, to be true to itself ("for my own name's sake") the Word must necessarily become flesh.

But before we reach that point - for it is the issue discussed in the next chapter - more must be said about the various forms through which Hebraic thought describes the content, the nature, and the activity of the divine Word. For although the various theophanies (occasions when God appears) occur in Israel's early period they are never relegated by later generations to being just examples of 'primitive thinking', to be replaced by a more intellectual grasp of what lay behind such pictorial thinking in the first place. In all the Rabbinical argumentation that was carried on in later centuries it was never forgotten that what they were doing was to seek to interpret the nature and revelatory purpose of God.

The Targums were translations of the Old Testament books into the Aramaic that was the common language of the Hebrew people in Palestine. They could be used in the Synagogue services in those areas where the folk were no longer able to follow the reading of the lessons in the original Hebrew. At times and in places they were more like imaginative expositions than word for word translations of the sacred and unalterable Hebrew text. The Targum to Psalm 137:7-8, for example, explains that Michael, the archangel, has the privilege of pleading with the Almighty for mercy for Israel. Again in the Apocalyptic literature he generally keeps this function (Daniel 10:21, 12:1; Jude 9) (de Lagarde, *Hagiographa Chaldaica*). Thus Michael is now being regarded as the successor, so to speak, of the Angel of Exodus 23:20, of whom it is said: "My name (my personality, the extension of my *nephesh*) is in him." Michael has thus become the *sar happanim*, "the chief of the angels of those who see the face of God", that is, the inmost circle.

By this time, and in the early centuries of the Christian Faith, 'God' was in danger of becoming lost behind a screen of concentric circles of angels in the seven heavens and so of becoming remote from mankind. He was in danger of becoming transcendent at the expense of the immanence of Old Testament thought, faith and experience. But he was saved from being lost to his world by the emphasis that the 'orthodox Judaism' of this late period made when it refused to let go of the theological nature and significance of the "Angel of the Covenant in whom is My Name".

Judaism held onto the basic meaning of the word 'angel', which is Hebrew for 'messenger'. Angels do not have wings, despite the vast number of syrupy Christmas cards and innumerable pictures of little winged cherubs that some unsophisticated people suppose represent reality. An angel is perhaps the sacramental parable on the level of human experience, or even at the level of the flesh, of the heavenly messengers of God "that do his will" (Psalm 104:4). We note how this is exemplified in all the records in all four Gospels in the case of the "young man" who guarded the empty tomb.

On the other hand the cherubim and seraphim, who undoubtedly had wings (six of them! Isaiah 6:2), as did the Sphinx in Egypt, were not angels of God. They were figments of the imagination of pluralistically minded people who lived round Israel's land. These 'beings' had been rendered captive (so some poetically minded theologies taught) by the Only God. He had put all things under his feet. These strange creatures must now serve the living God as instruments of his will, some even within the Holy of Holies.

So, back to the Angel of the Covenant - he now received a number of names. The most important of these was Metatron. Did that non-biblical word originally mean *meta*, with (God on his) throne? Was he an *hypostasis*, another substance, the unique essence of God but not God, or was he an intermediary between God and man? The word cannot derive from the Latin *medius*, mediating, as some believe. It is found, for example, in the Jewish Tractate *Sanhedrin* with reference to Exodus 24:1. There a heretic is mentioned; according to his logic he is desirous of worshipping Metatron as an intermediary (G.F.Moore, *Intermediaries in Jewish Theology*, pp.41-85). Actually, far from being derived from a word for 'mediator', the *metator* was an officer who went on ahead of a marauding army in order to select for the soldiers a halting place and quarters for the night. May we compare this comment on the word *metator* made by the Dutch Rabbi, Benjamin Mussafia, with John 14:2-7 as well as Exodus 23.20?

In 3 Enoch, a very late composition, long after the New Testament was complete, Metatron is accepted without question as "The Prince of the Presence", the angel who is the very 'Face' of God. Anything else, such as that Metatron was a kind of second God was regarded as "the worst of all possible heresies". This was because, as W. Eichrodt declares in his *Theology of the Old Testament* (I, p.7), "The angel is only a *nomen officii*, a *nomen naturae*; what we are permitted to see is that the angel performs the same function as God performs. The angel forgives sin even as God forgives sin. Thus the paradox is resolved in sacramental terms".

It is no surprise therefore to discover that the New Testament, being wholly a Hebraic document (except for just one sentence of Paul when he quoted an unknown Greek poet to his Greek audience in Athens, Acts 17:28!), gives compelling grounds for the doctrine of the nature of the God of the Hebrews to be formulated in trinitarian terms. The Word of God, spoken by God, the living God, and proceeding (alive) from the 'heart' of God, is the visible and audible performance of the will of God in action in the field of human endeavour. The Word is not a second God, as the Rabbis strongly emphasised, but is the One God being positively true to his name as Saviour. The Spirit of God is the Spirit of **God**; for God himself gives of himself, of his 'abundance', *perisseuma*, of his superfluity to mortal humanity: "You know him, because he abides with you, and he will be in you" (John 14:17).

All this was finally incorporated in the Nicene Creed in 325 CE. This is the name of the statement of belief which is still used in Christian worship. It covers succinctly the essentials of Christian belief, including the reality of the Incarnation and Resurrection of Christ, and the triune nature of the Godhead, and corresponds to the material of this chapter.

Chapter Four

THE INCARNATION OF CHRIST

What has all the discussion to date to do with the person of Christ? Christ belongs to the New Testament (or so we suppose, until we go farther in our quest) whereas our concern till now has been with the Old Testament alone. Curiously enough to obtain a bridge from the one Testament to the other we would be wise to return to the first verses of Genesis which we have already studied.

There in the beginning of God's creating he spoke the one word 'Light' - and light 'became'. That is to say, and thinking Hebraically, it issued from his 'heart', from the essence of his Being. Then it emerged through his mouth (remember the modern comic strip as an illustration of God's action), and finally it became an objectively discernible 'other' in the form of light. But more, it now continued to do the will of God, it gave light in a world of darkness and death. The light, directed by the 'living' God, acted as God's saving love, as the Light of God in creative action.

John's Gospel, consequently, when it seeks to tell us who Jesus is, begins at the same place as Genesis 1:1. John 1:1-3 runs: "In the beginning was the Word, and the Word was with God (in his 'heart'), and the Word was God." (Note, the Word is no 'thing', but is 'He', on the ground that God is the 'living' God of the Hebrew text of the Old Testament.) "He was in the beginning with God. All things came into being through him... What has come into being in him was life (the life of the living God), and the life was the light of all people." That is why John can write later of Christ: "I am the light of the world", that light that is the creative saving love of God for all peoples.

Straight away, however, we are up against a problem of meaning. For example, in non-Scriptural literature the concept of Light could cover a vast spectrum of meaning. The Dead Sea Scrolls, for one, describe the Qumran community as it refers to "us" as "Sons of light", and everyone else as "Sons of darkness". In the eyes of Jesus, however, their view of light was not 'of God': "You have heard that it was said, 'You shall love your neighbour and hate your enemy'". This was probably a dictum of the Community, for it does not occur in the Old Testament in so many words. Jesus continued, "But I say to you, love your enemies..." (Matthew 5:43). Jesus very likely on occasions met members of the Qumran Community, for some members paid occasional visits to the Temple, and he might have warned them that their understanding of light was not in conformity with that of Genesis.

Genesis has come down to us in the Hebrew language. We have already examined some of the peculiar Hebrew structures and learned how to accept them as vehicles capable of conveying even to modern society what its writers wished to express to their own generation. John's Gospel is written in Greek, a language which has no affiliation whatsoever with Hebrew. It has been a well-known fact to people trained in language all down the centuries that there are occasions where it is virtually impossible to transfer the meanings of some words expressed in one language accurately to another language, such as from ancient Hebrew into ancient Greek - and so into modern English.

We may digress to show how this is so in the case of one basic biblical term. Take the English word 'love'. Ask any happy young couple today if they know what love is, and they will laughingly try to describe it in words, perhaps even in poetry! Others may reply, "Yes, I know what love is, I love ice cream." But what they understand as love may not be what other cultures may believe it to be. Some central African tribes have no word at all for love in their language. It does not occur to them to 'marry for love'. In Hawaii the local people take for granted that their word *aloha* describes what the French *amour*, or the Latin *caritas* (English 'charity', 1 Corinthians 13 KJV) express. Hebrew does have the noun *ahabah* (plus its verbal root) for the natural affection of parents and children, and in fact the content of *ahabah* may be expressed by the New Testament Greek verbs *agapao* and *phileo*. But in the Hebrew of the Old Testament we are accosted with the unique term *hesed* for the content of the covenant relationship that binds Israel to God. In reality there is no equivalent term in either English or Greek, or, in fact, in any other language. This is because *hesed* speaks to us of God and is not employed by human persons for a relationship that our human lives can attain. The old KJV translates *hesed* by sixteen different English words. The RSV has reduced the number to four or five. When it appears in a merely human covenantal experience of one person to another, it may show itself simply as "kindness" (Micah 6:8). On the other hand, when faced with this basic term where it is used of God the RSV adheres by necessity to employing two English words used together to seek to express its 'covenantal' emphasis, *viz.* "steadfast love" (see, for example, Psalm 136); for there is an element of loyalty in it, of the faithfulness and devotion that is foremost in the wording of the popular hymn, "O love, that wilt not let me go."

In classical Greek literature there is no word that can carry the content of the word *hesed*. This is because it is used uniquely of the God of Israel, who acted it out in and upon his covenant people, Israel, freeing them from slavery, giving them a hope, sharing with them in all the vicissitudes of life together in their centuries-long pilgrimage. Being a fluent Greek speaker, Paul must have searched in his Greek literary heritage for a word to use for *hesed*. He found the noun *agape*, for by his day (as we now know) it was being inscribed in a number of pagan monuments only discovered in recent years (see Arndt and Gingrich, *A Greek Lexicon of the New Testament*, 1957, p.5). He chose *agape*, then, as the only ready term he could find to use in his 'Hymn to Love' in 1 Corinthians 13. But of course he did not succeed, and in part he had to describe love by what it is not!

Yet since *hesed* speaks to us of actions and not of passivity, the church has rightly used the language of Christian marriage to bring home to us what the love of the God of Israel can be for us; for the marriage covenant requires words of action between the parties - take, hold, promise, for better or worse, for richer or poorer, in sickness and in health, to love and to cherish, till death us do part. These are all terms embedded in the Hebrew word *hesed*. And then, remembering that love is an activity of the total *hesed*, the traditional Anglican service adds, "With my body I thee worship." In other words, the content of *hesed* is made known to us as a revelation of the mind of God in terms, not of a philosophical idea, but of actions of self-giving commitment in the physical world, and not just in mental intention.

We return to John's employment of the term 'Word', for it too can find no equivalent if it is to be translated from Hebrew to Greek. For the Greek noun *logos* which John uses was a very general term amongst the intellectuals of the Hellenistic world of his day. In the ordinary language of educated people *logos* might mean any one of these - speech, narrative, pronouncement, report, teaching, call, sense. "The Greek root *log-leg* represents to a comprehensive and overarching unity of meaning - gather, collect, select, report, speak" (H.Ritt, *Exegetical Dictionary of the New Testament*, Vol 2, p.357). Amongst philosophers, beginning with Heraclites of Ephesus (550-480 BCE), right on in European history until Hegel and Nietzsche in our era, *logos* has meant "the essential abiding law of the world, thought and custom" (*op. cit.*).

Some non-Jews who had been in contact with neighbouring Jewish thinkers might have imagined that they could speak of the *Logos* as an intermediary in creation between God and man, a kind of *tertium quid*, a term that more than one philosopher played with. We have seen by now, however, how greatly such philosophers misunderstood Hebraic thinking in this regard.

There is one particular writer we must pause to look at, however, for his influence upon his time was great. This was the Jewish philosopher, theologian and statesman Philo. His lifespan was roughly that of Jesus and the Apostle Paul. He knew little Hebrew, but was fluent in Greek and Latin and was proficient in the philosophy of the Greeks. In his numerous essays Philo attempted to show that the *Torah* is not just a book of stories and laws but a book of instructions for the soul. Philo's God is not the God of the *Torah*, who feels and acts on a human level, but is a God more like Plato's. He lays stress on interpreting to his contemporaries the significance of the *Logos*, the 'Word', that is the subject of the first chapter of John's Gospel. He rejects John's exegesis, however, and instead declares that true religion offers the possibility of 'seeing' God by ascending through the spheres, escaping the world of matter and arriving at the world of pure 'Form'. But because, as a believing Jew, he begins his argument with the words of Torah, held dear by both Jews and Christians, his influence until even long after his death, was something that more than a few of the Fathers had to war against. (This is further developed in my earlier book *From Moses to Paul: A Christological Study in the Light of our Hebraic Heritage*, pp.114ff.).

Others might suppose that here we have John using Platonic and Stoic concepts of the *Logos*, as his attempt to link universal and moral and religious experience with the Incarnation. No! There was no need to denigrate the true light, the *logos* that enlightens everyone which "was coming into the world" (John 1:9). Christ is all in all in himself:

> Though he was in the form of God,
> he did not regard equality with God
> as something to be exploited,
> but emptied himself,
> taking the form of a slave,
> being born in human likeness. (Philippians 2:6-7)

Here Christ as God is described in very personal terms. Likewise, what Logos means for John includes being a person, truly human, for true personhood is at the centre of Reality, or Truth; for the Truth is that God is the supreme Person.

Today we have inserted this root *log* into the names of many scientific categories of study; we find it in Zoology, Pathology, Physiology, Geology, and so on. In other words the concept of Logos is accepted today as having affinity primarily with the world of the sciences, all of which, it is believed, give us a handle on ultimate reality and the meaning of human existence. In this image, however, *logos* is an impersonal concept.

A.C. Bouquet, in his ground-breaking work published in 1959, *The Christian Faith and Non-Christian Religions*, states:

> Continental Protestantism starts, no doubt, with a prejudice against linking the Johannine Logos with Hellenistic ideas. Be that as it may, John was writing for Greek-speaking Gentiles, so surely he meant it to be understood both as Neoplatonic and as Hebraic, just as we have evangelical and theological interpretations of the Cross today.

For Bouquet then, *logos* was Neo-platonic and Hellenistic. The Church Father Tertullian, the African who had been brought up as a Stoic, was teaching in the year 197 CE that the *Logos* is the "immanent Reason of the world". This is real Neoplatonic language. Other theologians saw the *Logos* as God's continual process in the realms of the Spirit. But the whole New Testament proclaims that in Christ we have one full manifestation in the flesh, of God coming to bring about human redemption by building the kingdom around himself on earth as in heaven.

We cannot evade the fact that John begins his description of the *Logos* by setting it in comparison with what we read in the first verses of Genesis. He has the Septuagint before him as well as the Hebrew text; it offers him a ready-made translation into Greek. "Let light become, and light became, *egeneto*". So he employs the same Greek verb when he comes to the words "The Word became, *egeneto*, flesh." But in quoting Genesis he wishes to anchor his exegesis in the Hebraic approach to the area of the divine which as we have seen is unique. He does not deny, nor seek to refute, the many possible interpretations which the Hellenistic intelligentsia of his day might read into his particular employment of the word *Logos*; it may be that he even believed Christ was also all these philosophical ideas and more at once. What he is doing above all is affirming that there is but one ultimate content to the term 'Word', and that content is divine being, one with God himself.

John now expresses (v.6ff.), in lateral thinking, what he believes is important for his readers to learn as he leads us to take our eyes off 'heaven' and bring them down to 'earth'. He prepares us to make this move by informing us of "a man sent from God", *viz.* John the Baptist. He, we learn, was not that heavenly light mentioned in v.4, "but he came to testify to the light". It certainly needed such an attestation, for what comes next is so ludicrous, so absurd, so incongruous and contrary to natural beliefs about God that it is not surprising to learn that only some "believed in his 'Name'" (a very anthropomorphic and non-Platonic idea!). And then comes the equally astonishing statement that "he gave [them] power to become children of God."

This 'prologue' to the Gospel culminates in a statement which both the world of his day and the world ever since have rejected as destructive of all religious thought and awareness about the mystery of the divine. It is stated in just one short phrase. It seems to shatter all belief in the concept of a Creator Spirit before whom humankind can but bow in awe and fear. It runs: "The Word became flesh."

Does this mean that the divine became a human being, the *nephesh* of a Semitic male, a member of our sinful human family of frail, short-lived creatures of a day? Does it mean that the Word of God, God's speech, his *dabar*, uttered from the heart of his very self, became effective, active, lovingly active, creatively and purposefully vital in the sphere of human life on earth, and, in the structure of a mere human *nephesh*, actually lived in a remote province of the mighty Roman Empire called Galilee? ("Can any good come out of Galilee?" people jibed in those days.) John affirms just that!

He goes on further:

> From his fullness (remember, the Word is of God and bears, not part of God, not just his breath, which conveys the spoken word, but all of God, all of his wholeness, his *pleroma*) we have all received grace upon grace... No one has ever seen God. It is God's only Son, who is close to the Father's heart, who has made him known.

That then is what 'Incarnation' means. This is the fulfilment of covenant, this is the meaning of grace.

We have just read that the *Logos* was the conveyor of the grace of God, and that it was grace that opened the eyes of some to see God's glory; and glory, we recall, is the anthropomorphic term for God's 'outer clothing', as it were. But now, when the Word became flesh (v.14), this glory was being worn by a human being. When Jesus was 'glorified' in the Transfiguration scene, he was glorified in his humanity - it was not simply that the disciples became aware of his divinity.

A pointer to discovering the manner in which God works, which he gives us, step by step, in the garb of pictorial theology, is how we human creatures are able to visualise what incarnation means. At Judges 6:12 we have a story that spells it out, stage by stage. The Midianite army is threatening Israel. God makes use of "the angel of the LORD" to address the young soldier, Gideon, in the words, "The LORD is with you" (the 'with' being used in the sense of the phrase *Im-ma-nu-el*, With-us-is-God (Isaiah 8:8). Then the LORD says to Gideon (not any longer, we note, the angel of the LORD), "Go in this might of yours (his human strength) and deliver Israel". Gideon responds to God's call by offering up, at God's instigation (for all is of grace) a flesh and flour sacrifice, thereby demonstrating his willingness to be used by God. Thereupon the spirit of the LORD clothed himself with Gideon (Judges 6:34, RSV "took possession of Gideon"), whereupon Gideon sounded the trumpet. Gideon's small army of one hundred men, carefully selected under God's guidance, thereupon rout the Midianites "without a shot being fired" to use our modern idiom. Who then won the battle? Was it God? Or was it Gideon? Was it not rather God in Gideon?

Here we have an instance of the Hebrew Bible's use of 'anthropomorphism' in relation to God. This word means, "representing, describing, thinking of, God in terms of human beings", with human attributes and characteristics. The Greek Septuagint translation, made about 250 BCE in the Gentile city of Alexandria, Egypt, usually sought to avoid translating the anthropomorphisms of the Hebrew language, regarding them as rather naive! If so, then Jesus' parable of the Two Sons (Luke 15:11-24) is also naive. Incidentally, 'anthropopathic' is the term used to apply to the Godhead the ability to suffer pain even as humankind suffers.

In a previous chapter we mentioned how God could place his glory upon his own chosen people. At this point in his exegesis of *Logos* John now refers back to this version of God's glory in the body of Israel, his 'son'. He writes: "The Word became flesh and lived among us, and we have seen his glory, the glory as of a father's only son." The Greek word means literally that the Word 'tabernacled' amongst us, that he pitched his tent on our site. And this in turn reminds us what God did during the Exodus when he 'camped' amongst his people in the cloud over the tabernacle.

John wishes to emphasise that the Word of God had 'descended' from the realm of the Spirit and had become, no longer a mental image, no longer a philosophical idea, but a human being in history. He referred back to what God, so long before, in the days of Egypt, had ordered Moses to say to Pharaoh, "Thus says the LORD, Israel is my first-born son" (Exodus 4:22).

Here we find no discussion on metaphysical lines on the relationship between the divine and the human. Rather, John can declare quite daringly "the glory of a father's only son". And similiarly in concrete terms he describes Jesus as being "full of grace and truth". The human son, whom we know as Jesus, through the descent of the Word to our human level, is full of grace, even as God himself is, so that he is also the Truth itself, even as God is. Then, in v.18, to cap it all, he reiterates the whole Old Testament witness in these words: "No one has ever seen God. It is God's only Son, who is close to the Father's heart, who has made him known." Or, as the post-resurrection language of John 14:7 declares: "If you know me, you will know my Father also".

Today's world finds it difficult to accept the story of creation as it is in Genesis, because it seems to be "just another of the many myths that abound, even in Central Africa and in the islands of the Pacific". Myths abound because, when confronted by mystery the human race seeks a myth to provide a satisfactory explanation of the origin of all things. But those faithful persons who have left us with the Genesis stories travelled on a completely different road.

There is a sense in which the book of Exodus comes before the book of Genesis. Exodus tells us how God had brought a rabble of slaves into being as an ordered society of God-conscious human beings. He had spoken the Word to Moses, "Go", as he had done to Abraham, "Go", (Genesis 12:1). In the power of that word Moses went, because God had added "I will be with you" (Exodus 3:12). "I will be" is the same one word by which God next informs Moses who he is, *viz.* I AM (v.14). The power of Egypt is more than a mere mythical monster, it is a stark and dark reality; as such it is representative of the terrors of the chaotic waters of the primal deep. God becomes known to Moses as *Yahweh*, the third personal form of the one word of divine revelation, *ehyeh*, I AM.

So God had actually, historically speaking, created Israel, as he had created heaven and earth, out of chaos, now perhaps moral chaos, and he had done so by being with his chosen people as their Saviour from the powers of darkness, by his mysterious yet all-loving creative Presence in their experience of life. So God promised to be with Moses and send him to overcome the dark powers of oppression and moral chaos ('bricks without straw'). Yahweh brings his people freedom and order out of their chaos. That understanding of actual deliverance in history now became the model for understanding creation.

The appropriate word to be used in connection with 'the road travelled' by the authors of both Genesis and Exodus is 'grace', for grace represents the love of God incarnate in his saving initiative. John now interpolates this word at this point (John 1:14) to exegete this new genesis and exodus in the coming of Christ. And by the same grace, sinful men and women could learn to call this Jesus the Son of God, a step beyond what they knew of sonship from the Old Testament - when Israel had been named Son of God (Exodus 4:22) or when Israel's later kings, each in turn representing the nation of Israel in the line of David had also been called "Son of God" (Psalm 2:7).

The title "Son of ..." can mean many things, in fact the name of each member of the family in a Semitic culture can be employed in various ways. We recall "Father of mercies..." as a description of God. In Arabic culture one may describe a very great battle as "the mother of all battles", showing that gender really has nothing to do with it. Yet nothing can be closer than the personal relationships within a family. The title Word of God is therefore not enough. 'Son of God', (or 'Daughter', as with Wisdom in Proverbs 8), brings in a new personal dimension to the divine-human relationship, God relating personally to men and women and vice versa.

William Johnstone has written of the books of Chronicles:

> The chronicler has presented the House of David as the means whereby the sovereignty of God can be realised among all the nations of the world. The status of the king of the House of David has been expounded in sacramental terms. He sits on no merely human throne but on the throne of the Lord: he is the visible expression in physical terms of the cosmic sovereignty of God (e.g. 1 Chronicles 28:5). Likewise the people of Israel [Son of God] are the Lord's host on earth, the counterpart in the physical sphere of the hosts of the Lord in the cosmic sphere. (1 Chronicles 11:9)

David here is the 'son of God' in whom God is present to his people. John's argument now leads us to discover why Jesus accepted gladly the title 'Son of David' that his contemporaries bestowed upon him. The Gospel writers (Matthew 1:6; Luke 1:69; 3:23,31), by converging routes, claim Jesus to be descended from, and so to be 'son of' David. Jesus was certainly brought up in the village synagogue to learn from the local Rabbi (for Messianism was in the air at the time) what he would then go on to read for himself in Chronicles. Again we reiterate that Jesus was a Jew, brought up in the atmosphere of Hebraic thinking, and discovering things for himself about God when even still only a boy of twelve, as in the passage from Luke 2.4ff. which ends with the words: "And Jesus increased in wisdom and in years, and in divine and human favour".

From the book of Psalms the young Jesus would learn that king David, and his successors on the throne in Jerusalem, were thought of as the 'head of the body' of Israel, and thus the representative of the people to God, and the spokesman of God to the people. Psalm 2:6-8 runs:

> I have set my king in Zion, my holy hill... he said to me,
> "You are my son, today have I begotten you. Ask of me, and
> I will make the nations your heritage".

This, and more, was the heritage of one whom Pilate would ultimately name "Jesus of Nazareth, the King of the Jews" without having any real awareness of what he was saying (John 19:19).

Similarly the chief priest, like each Son of David, was intermediary between his people and God. This was witnessed to by his wearing an ephod, on which were attached the names of the twelve tribes of Israel. This meant that when he approached the Holy Place of the

Presence, he was acting as their mediator to God, carrying in with him the names of all twelve tribes. Then at the conclusion of the sacrificial service he blessed the people from God, using the very words of the Lord. It is noticeable that when Jesus chose disciples "to be with him" he chose twelve, and all of them males. Jesus never had any thought of giving the world a 'new religion', his purpose was to continue, but with a new dimension, the work of God in God's employment of the Old Testament kings and priests who are now rolled together in Jesus.

Men called Jesus 'Son of God'; he did not 'snatch' at divinity for himself (Philippians 2:6-8), on the contrary he "emptied himself, taking the form of a slave, being born in human likeness". The title he gave to himself was 'Son of Man'. In contrast with the title 'Son of God', no one, male nor female, gave him this title, it was his own name for himself, the phrase being found exclusively on the lips of Jesus, some 80 times in all, though it occurs once again, in Acts 7:26, after Jesus' death.

In the Greek of the New Testament the phrase always occurs as 'the Son of Man'. This unusual phraseology, however, reveals what Jesus meant by employing it. 'Son of' can have a number of meanings other than that of being the biological son of a particular father; principally it can mean one who fully represents another, who is greater than himself, in person. But also, as we have already noted, 'the man' ('the' being the generic article, as in the phrase children are taught at school "the horse is a noble animal") is a quotation from Genesis 1:27: "And God (plural) created (*bara*, the verb in the singular that is used of God's actions alone) *eth ha-adam*, man, humankind (not one male person called Adam, but humanity in both sexes, male and female (this fact now emphasised by the repetition of "he created them"); so, as the NRSV renders this significant verse: "So God created humankind in his image, in the image of God he created them; male and female he created them". In this sense Jesus is calling himself 'the man', the representative of the human race.

Many scholars have struggled to understand what Jesus meant by calling himself "Son of Man". (For a full discussion see: *Jesus Son of man: A Fresh Examination of the Son of Man Sayings in the Gospels in the Light of Recent Research*, by Barnabas Lindars SSF, SPCK, 1983; or, *The Son of Man in the teaching of Jesus*, by A.J.B. Higgins, C.U.P. 1980). Some have suggested that it was a humble way of saying "I", as a person might say, "yours truly was present at the scene", thus representing his selflessness and self-abnegation, and there are still more theories. But if we begin with phrases available to Jesus from his Hebraic heritage we can find two reasons for his choice which belong together 'like two sides of a coin'.

In himself, as a human baby, he was 'created' (a word we can use of the birth of any baby) in the image of God. Just as God cannot be defined in terms of sex, neither here can Jesus. He was humanity in essence, he was the ultimate representative of the human race. As such he was the new 'son' of the plural God, the image of the God who had created mankind in two sexes, come to reveal in human flesh, not the Being of God, but the creative, redemptive and saving love of the living God, at the human level, at the level that the plural 'male and female' have, not separately but in common.

This is exemplified in the two accounts of Genesis. As we have noted already, it is sin, and sin only, which destroys the unity of the human *nephesh*. Now the authors of both ancient documents, whom we call J and P, come at the issue of creation from different angles - as do the authors of the first three gospels and the author of the fourth gospel come at the issue of the person of Christ; but both talk about the nature of humankind before the entry of sin. In the first 'theological picture' of creation, human beings and the command to them to be fruitful come before sin even existed (Genesis 1). In the second 'theological picture', the unity of 'Mr Adam' and 'Mrs Eve' (Genesis 2) describes the ideal nature of humankind, again before the 'Fall'. "She is bone of my bones and flesh of my flesh" Adam exclaims; so "they became one flesh", says Genesis 2:23-24. All Jesus' hearers would be so acquainted with the Genesis stories that they could readily recognise what Jesus was claiming for himself in using this unique title: in calling himself the son of Man, he was describing himself as the heir of both Adam and Eve.

But there is more in the biblical witness with which the inhabitants of both Nazareth and Jerusalem would be familiar. There was the vision of Daniel in the book of that name at Daniel 7:1-14. This vision became vivid to Daniel in the reign of the abominable King Belshazzar at the period when the Israelites were groaning under the rule of this violent Persian monarch. What we can read today and what Jesus undoubtedly read in the scroll kept in the 'Ark' in his local village Synagogue was a double vision expressed in verse. First, there was the sight of an "Ancient One" (Daniel 7:9-10 NRSV, "the Ancient of Days" KJV, as the original Aramaic has it) taking his seat on his throne of judgement. Then separately follows Daniel's second vision: "I saw one like a human being, (NRSV, one like 'a son of man' in the original Aramaic), like 'the Son of Man' (KJV, the form that has taken hold upon today's popular theologising) coming with the clouds of heaven". Then vv.13-14 proceed: "He came to the Ancient One (NRSV) and was presented before him. To him was given dominion and glory and kingship... his dominion is an everlasting dominion that shall not pass away..."

It is true that this Danielic vision has become the majority view of the origin of Jesus' calling himself 'Son of Man', with the emphasis on his "coming in the clouds of heaven". But, true to his own Hebraic heritage, it is surely almost certain that Jesus thought in terms of both heaven and earth together, for in Old Testament thought there is only one created universe, in which heaven and earth belong together. Heaven does not exist without earth, and earth does not exist without heaven. And since human life is on earth, and earth is the focus of the Bible, then in that sense the heavens exist for the earth. Sun and moon are pictured as being made to throw light on the earth. So, both Genesis and Daniel contributed to Jesus naming himself Son of Man. His doing so has given us one of the best theological pictures of what we mean when we speak of the Incarnation of the Son of God. For he is both true human and true God.

There is one factor, however, that links together the contents of the title Son of David with that of Son of Man, and that is the reality of sin. The outsider might consider it strange of Jesus to link himself to such a blatant sinner as David turned out to be. The book of Leviticus classifies sins into two groups. First, there are the ordinary everyday sins that are common to human nature. For these the cult provides means of atonement through a range of sacrifices. Second, however, there are two groups of sins for which there is only the death penalty available. These are adultery and murder. They are described as "sins with a high hand". So named they are described like so much else in the Old Testament theological writings by means of a telling picture. Its title in Leviticus invites us to see the hand raised high to strike, or, if you like, the picture, not of an inadvertent act, but of a deliberately planned and thought out act of destructive wickedness. Murder kills the body without touching the 'soul' (as Gentiles understand the term), thereby splitting the wholeness of a human *nephesh*. Adultery, rape, sodomy destroy the psyche of the sufferer, and even that of the perpetrator as well, and therefore also destroy the wholeness of the *nephesh*.

The new evil created here is the destruction of the unity of the creature God has created. It reveals itself clearly in acts of adultery. Sexual union between a man and a woman is in reality the physical expression of his and her total ('whole') self-giving, the one to the other, in mutual love of the whole person, the *nephesh*, the spirit. It can and is meant to be 'very heaven', to use the popular phrase. Jewish tradition speaks of the loving, caring, creative Presence of God as hovering over the marriage bed as God's *Shekhinah*. The root of this word is what John uses at John 1:14: "The Word became flesh and *sh-kh-an* among us", hovered over, rested, dwelt in love and care. But sexual sins witness that love may become lust, joy may become apathy, satisfaction may become greed and dominance. Human unity of flesh and spirit can be shattered.

David committed both of these acts. He raped Bathsheba, and he ordered the murder of her husband. But in later life David had become a sincere penitent, and is portrayed as a forgiven sinner. As such he was born again to be a new person by the power and grace of God. Consequently then, since Jesus knew that he had come, not just to preach the Good News, but to act out what God acts out, in taking on himself the name of David he was taking on himself his calling to be Saviour not just of such as David but of the whole world array of sinful human beings. In this way he revealed that he was the true image of God, for saving, forgiving love and recreative passion is at the heart of God.

In the city of Debrecen in Hungary there is housed in a special room of the city museum and art gallery a vast canvas, the work of the Hungarian painter Munkacsy; the canvas fills the whole top end of the large gallery where it is exhibited alone. The artist portrays Jesus as the Suffering Servant bowing in agony before Pontius Pilate. Behind Pilate stands a leering crowd. Around the stooping figure of Jesus converges the inhuman Roman soldiery. We see them smashing down on Jesus' head the crown of thorns. The blood runs down his neck and face and drips onto his torn and agonised body. He can scarcely stand after the flogging he has received, the leather thongs studded with rusty nails having torn the flesh of his back. And it is then, as he gazed in exasperated horror at his silent victim that Pilate uttered those two famous words *"Ecce homo"*. Munkacsy believed in the true Hebraic tradition, that in painting a picture of Jesus the man, he was painting a picture of God.

These two Latin words are difficult to render in English. Latin does not possess either the definite article 'the' or the indefinite 'a'. "Behold the man" is the rendering we have inherited from the King James Version of the Bible. Modern versions are each in their own way intent on laying bare the basic meaning of the words. The RSV has "Here is the man", so also both the NRSV and the Jerusalem Bible. The Contemporary English Version suggests rather "Look at the man!", while the Good News Bible expands to "Look! Here is the man".

But none of the renderings is fully able to interpret for us these two Latin words. Was Pilate not saying "Look, that is the man for you", so that his Jewish attendants, knowing their Bible as Pilate did not, perhaps almost unconsciously mumbled in reply, "Yes, and in his broken humanity God has been wiped out"? But later, Paul could say in his second Corinthian letter (5:19), "God was in Christ [at that moment when he bowed in agony before Pilate] reconciling the world to himself".

As 'Son of Man', then, Jesus himself has summed up the significance of what we call the Incarnation. In all the horror and devastation of soul Jesus experienced under Pilate, and in the agony of both mind and body he underwent a few hours later on the Cross, our Hebraic view of the Incarnation declares to us that the whole Godhead, in Christ, so entered into the ultimate experience that humanity could possibly undergo, that the whole Godhead, in Christ, voiced the appalling cry, "My God, why hast thou forsaken me".

The Hebraic understanding of the Incarnation has more to reveal to us concerning the nature of God. We look at Jesus' usage of the words *ego eimi*, "It is I", or, on a number of occasions, translated as "I am". This could on occasions reveal his one-ness with the God who told Moses to inform the Israelites, "I AM, *ehyeh*, has sent me to you" (Exodus 3:14). There was the occasion when Jesus walked on the Sea of Galilee to meet his disciples, caught in a storm as they were. What happened was that "they were terrified, saying, 'It is a ghost!'. And they cried out in fear. But immediately Jesus spoke to them and said: 'Take heart, it is I, (*ego eimi, ehyeh*); do not be afraid'" (Matthew 14:26-27; Mark 6:50).

This incident shows us the substance of the Incarnation. Jesus' reply, "It is I" could indeed be the meaning of the phrase here, in fact it could be the only meaning. Yet we are told that the disciples were literally transfixed with horror in that they found themselves in the presence of the numinous, overcome by an overwhelming sense of mystery and dread - of the God they were accustomed to sing about at worship, the God of the storm, earthquake and whirlwind (Psalm 107:23-26):

> Some went down to the sea in ships,
> doing business on the mighty waters;
> they saw the deeds of the LORD,
> his wondrous works in the deep.
> For he commanded and raised the stormy wind,
> which lifted up the waves of the sea...
> Their courage melted away in their calamity;
> they reeled and staggered like drunkards,
> and were at their wits' end.
> > Then they cried to the LORD in their trouble...
> > he made the storm be still...

A great windstorm arose, so that the boat was already being swamped. But he was in the stern, asleep on a cushion; and they woke him up and said to him, "Teacher, do you not care that we are perishing?" He woke up and rebuked the wind, and said to the sea, "Peace! Be still!" Then the wind ceased, and there was a dead calm. (Mark 4:37-39)

This was the same Jesus who had said before, "I AM". Compare Mark 13:6, 14:62; Luke 22:70; and five times also in John's Gospel; and see also Deuteronomy 32:39; Isaiah 43:10. He also made the overwhelming utterance, "Before Abraham was, I AM" (John 8:58).

Few of the Church Fathers in the early Christian centuries had any knowledge of Hebrew. One exception was the great biblical scholar, Irenaeus, bishop of Lyons (130-200 CE), and another in the following century was Cyprian, who, about 255 CE opposed those Nestorians who dabbled with a dualistic view of the nature of Christ. When Pope Damasus, in the year 382, invited the scholar Jerome to make a translation of the whole Bible into the common (vulgar) tongue of the Roman Empire, he produced, after 20 years work, the rendering that became known as the Vulgate. Jerome knew Greek well and so was able to tackle the New Testament. But by the time he had completed it he had become intensely aware that to translate the Old Testament only from the Greek Septuagint was not good enough. So he humbly sat at the feet of Jewish scholars living in Rome; eventually he was able to produce his translation in Latin that was more nearly true to its 'Hebraic' nature than if he had stayed with the Septuagint alone. He did an immense service to the Church as a whole, because, with the Vulgate Old Testament in their hands, most Latin Fathers became able to 'feel' the manner in which the Old Testament writers handled their material.

This helped to consolidate the victory in the *homoousios-homoiousios* controversy for those who could confidently proclaim the 'oneness' of the person of Christ with the Father. The issue at stake was whether Jesus was 'of one substance' with the Father (*homoousios*), or just 'of like substance' (*homoi-ousios*). Once that issue was decided, the Creeds could be standardised and then disseminated.

The Council of Chalcedon, then, produced the doctrine of hypostatic union, which is the affirmation that in Jesus Christ the divine and human natures are united in one Person without any kind of separation or confusion. This union was for a purpose, seen through the utterance of the Word and the activity of the Spirit. We can understand the Fathers pointing out to one another the validity of Genesis 1:31 - the creation was not just good, it was good for a purpose, for God's plan for the redemption of the cosmos. And in the Centre of the whole mighty and emerging plan we meet with the Christ made incarnate, the 'operator' of God's plan of redemption.

There are those today who speak of the 'myth' of the Incarnation; others declare the Incarnation impossible, as if one hoped to walk by placing both feet in the one shoe. But the Hebraic metaphor of the coin illuminating the many ways in which God kept on revealing himself throughout the whole Old Testament period, that is, even before the birth of Christ, illustrates clearly what John meant when he wrote "The Word became flesh, and dwelt among us". Consequently, if now we substitute for the plain word 'coin' the ecclesiastical term 'sacrament', we discover that Jesus is the sacrament, the Real Presence, under the sign of his humanity, of a redeeming Presence that was in the world from the creation of all things.

One of the issues the Church Fathers had to face here was an aspect of the Hellenistic world view to which we drew attention in the Introduction. This was the notion that the body is, by its very nature, evil. Oriental religions have, of course, made the most of this idea. Many western Christians even today take a dim view of the body in all its parts and passions - and the Church has a very poor track record indeed in its attitudes to sex.

Christian theology informs us that God made the body, that God loves it, and that God took it to himself in the womb of Mary (see *The Romance of the Word*, by Robert Farrar Capon, Eerdmans, 1995, p.104). The flesh as such is not evil, nor is it, alone, the seat of evil. The root of evil in the New Testament is in the mind, and it is through being "alienated in our minds" that our whole selves, body and soul, disintegrate and are characterised as 'flesh'. Thus all human beings, each of whom is a whole united *nephesh*, are sinners, and all are alienated from God; all therefore must be rescued, and that can be done by God alone (Genesis 3:24). Towards the end of Jesus' crucifixion, the pain and the agony of mind and body must have reached beyond human imagination. Yet at that point in the gospel narrative, in the midst of bodily disintegration, and out of divine love, Jesus uttered another prayer even as he gazed out at the leering crowd: "Father, forgive them, for they do not know what they are doing" (Luke 23:34).

We refer back to what Leviticus tells us about the double classification of sins. There was the one grouping of "sins of inadvertence", of "they know not what they do", and there was the second grouping of "sins with a high hand", and that must of course include crucifixion of an innocent victim. So Jesus is in effect saying - as with the young King David, who committed both murder and adultery - that even these sins are forgivable. Consequently even the ultimate sin of murdering the Son of God was, in Jesus' sight, in the category of the forgivable.

So we are now presented with a miracle of revelation. The incarnate Son, through this spoken word of love, care and compassion, had now brought into human life in space and time the eternal Word of the living triune God. This was the ultimate assurance that God was there and then forgiving the ultimate sin that humanity could commit, regarding it as being merely a weakness of the flesh, while the leering crowd were miserably unaware that they in their turn had incurred the death penalty designated in Leviticus.

Since it has been Incarnation alone that has revealed this majestic, creative, suffering, forgiving love of the living God at one particular moment in space and time, it does not mean that God has waited, so to speak, from all eternity, to act out his redemptive plan only through the Cross of Christ. In eternity, time does not happen as we experience it on earth: "A thousand years in your sight are like yesterday when it is past" (Psalm 90:4). "God is the same, yesterday, today and forever". "I am Alpha and Omega, the beginning and the end". "I the Lord do not change" (Malachi 3:6). Of Jesus: "Before Abraham was I AM".

What we discover therefore from the utterances of Jesus from the Cross is that he himself was at that moment in our time performing the one and only act of redemption that empowered the salvation of all humankind. There have been many theories that seek to define exactly what Jesus accomplished for us humans and for our salvation by his sufferings and death on the Cross in the year 33 CE. One non-Hebraic, but very Hellenistic theory that has raised its head more than once in history is that in Christ God 'did a deal' with the Devil to rescue us from death and hell.

But the Cross was no transaction with the devil or any other being, it was revelation of the serving, loving, creative nature of the ever-living God. Our triune God is eternally the Saviour, eternally suffering 'hell' at the antics of his perverted but beloved sons and daughters (Hosea 11:8-9). Only, at one point in history, God finally answered the cry of his suffering, beloved, chosen people, which was: "O that you would tear open the heavens and come down... to make your Name [of 'Saviour', as Isaiah had declared] known to your adversaries" (Isaiah 64:1-2). And this is exactly what God did by choosing the way of Incarnation. Now the eternally unchanging, redemptive, compassionate, forgiving, steadfast love of the eternal creator God has been revealed for all time and in all places, for in the obedience and action of Christ this eternal love became incarnated in the body of humanity. God spoke and it was done. "So shall my Word be that goes out from my mouth; it shall not return to me empty, but it shall accomplish that which I purpose, and succeed in the thing for which I sent it" (Isaiah 55:11). "I am the Way, the Truth, and the Life", Jesus said to his inner group of very human disciples (John 14:6).

It is only because of the Incarnation that we learn that this committed, forgiving love is in reality the Truth of our triune God, that it has been so from all ages, and that it will be so till time finally merges into eternity. For it all depended on Christ, the Centre. That was why, just moments before he died, Jesus could exclaim in absolute relief, trust and gratification, "It is finished". These words we find at John 17:4, "I have glorified you on earth by finishing the work [the word used at Genesis 2:2] that you gave me to do".

In the light of this dramatic declaration of Jesus, it is not surprising that, while not denying it, he did not encourage people to call him Messiah. Should they do so they would be putting the wrong content into the term, one that spoke of military might and of dictatorship. Many, including the Jewish population living in the Roman Empire, looked for just this in their coming 'redeemer'. The term 'Messiah' in Hebrew means 'anointed', that is to say anointed to office, such as that of a king. In New Testament Greek 'anointed' is translated as *christos*, the name by which most Christians in the world actually know Jesus and worship him, and from which, moreover, the name 'Christian' is derived. This curious fact reminds us, or should do so, of the mystery enshrined in the Incarnation; it reminds us that the all-holy God chooses to act and reveal himself; in the Old Testament he put his Spirit in a certain human being, his anointed - be they kings or priests - while in the New Testament he actually becomes a human being who is anointed in the fullest possible way with the Spirit.

Two quotations remind us of the importance of the Old Testament and Hebraic thinking in order to understand the divine purpose. One is the short phrase attributed to a number of writers:

How odd of God to choose the Jews!

to which was added:

Yet not so odd as those who choose
a Jewish God, and spurn the Jews!

The other is the story that King Frederick the Great of Prussia once asked his court chaplain to give him just one proof of the existence of God. To which the chaplain replied, "Sire, the Jews".

Both quotations point to the fact that God acts and makes himself known in a very concrete and direct way, first in the history of Israel and ultimately in its fulfilment in Christ.

Chapter Five

THE RESURRECTION

Pinchas Lapide, the Jewish scholar, in *The Resurrection of Jesus: A Jewish Perspective*, writes:

> The New Testament reports about the resurrection of Christ follow naturally from the Hebrew and Old Testament view. It is as rooted in Judaism that it became one of the articles of faith; it is mentioned in the Talmud (Sanhedrin X, 1) and became one of the 13 articles of faith of the Jewish sage Maimonides (1135-1204). (pp.58,62)

In Lapide's thought, resurrection is explicitly contrasted with the immortality of the soul. For him there is the idea of the former in Judaism, but none whatever of the latter. And he says that the idea of resurrection came out of the cradle of Judaism:

> For Hebraic theology never held to the idea of the immortality of the soul, in fact the Hebrew bible has no place even for the existence of the soul.

So much for the witness of a Jewish scholar; now we turn to a great Christian theologian, Karl Barth. Most of Barth's monumental theology saw the light in the years he taught at Basel in Switzerland. Throughout those years Walter Eichrodt too taught and wrote his profoundly important Theology of the Old Testament in Basel. The two men were great friends, and each sat at the feet of the other, so to speak. Barth at one point in his life declared that there is no need to examine problems around the empty tomb, or discuss the miraculous, for these are problems merely for historical criticism; the various appearances cannot scientifically, and, humanly speaking, be assessed and arranged in order, nor be proved as mere legends or myths. The empty tomb in itself, except for John 20:8, does not evoke faith, which could have been reached later in retrospect by John.

Yet unless Christ's resurrection was of the body, we have no guarantee that it was in fact the "decisively-acting Subject, Jesus himself, who rose from the dead" (*Church Dogmatics III 2*, p.448). For Barth, the logic of resurrection followed from the logic of incarnation.

This is because our faith is rooted in the fact of the historical Christ. But what can we say about the non-scientifically-verifiable elements in the gospel stories? Are they too facts of history? Can we accept as facts what we are told of the birth and resurrection of Jesus? What help can we receive here from the 'Hebraic' thinking of the two Testaments? It was just because of Old Testament thought that Barth recognised the basic significance of the Resurrection, and how it was the centre point of the whole Christian affirmation.

In our science-based culture it is easy for supposedly enlightened people to suggest that the 'material' appearances of the risen Christ can be explained away in terms of psychology, or of wishful thinking. Or it may be thought that the devastating experience of actually witnessing the death of Jesus left simple folk in such a state of shock that they could not let go their involvement with the Jesus they had worshipped, and so simply continued in faith to worship him as they broke bread together and reminded each other of all that Jesus had said and done. But if you fail to take the restoration of bodily reality seriously (which is what resurrection is about), then you fail to appreciate the strength and significance of the Old Testament view of the reality and goodness of the body. Modern science here is actually in line with Old Testament insights and not against them.

There are even high-minded people today who reject the stories of the Christ, both as Jesus of Nazareth, and as the risen Christ, which tell of his eating the flesh of fish. This view arises from their modern philosophical stance that a person of Spirit should be a vegetarian. "Get up, Peter, kill and eat", were words of invitation to Peter that seemed to come from heaven (Acts 10:13). Peter's negative reply was based not on vegetarian principles but upon the religious scruples of his period. "By no means, Lord, for I have never eaten anything that is profane or unclean". The voice said to him again, a second time, "What God has made clean, you must not call profane". In other words eating food, including meat, was a natural and divinely sanctioned human activity.

Whatever we make of the argument that only after the Fall did humans cease to be vegetarian, here we are told that God has provided all living creatures for the sustenance of humankind. Consequently, as Son of Man Jesus shared in that sustenance. Eating with his disciples in Galilee has as its *aharith* an eschatological significance, his eating with them in the life to come, a natural element in the Hebraic faith; for there his chosen ones will be as fully whole persons as they were in their days on earth. What we are seeing in the eating on earth is the eternal meaning of a moment in history.

In 1 Corinthians 15, Paul, as a "Hebrew of Hebrews" (his own expression), declares emphatically that the dead in Christ are not mere naked 'souls'. In his day, as in ours, many sophisticated people, ignoring, even despising, the body, believed in some kind of future in eternity for the souls of humanity. Thus it is that today the concept of the transmigration of souls gains much popular support. "In a previous life I was Mary Queen of Scots. In the next life I hope I shall be someone of consequence; I deserve it", and so on. No, says Paul, we are to realise that there is resurrection of the dead, because of the resurrection of Christ. Our human body dies, because it is of perishable material, but it is raised of imperishable substance, that is to say, it will be a glorious body; it will be a spiritual body - this means a body alive by the Spirit, not something less than a body, or a 'non-material body' (a contradiction in terms). The physical human body is sown in the ground, in the grave (like a seed); it is raised a spiritual body (vv.42-44). In other words, in non-scientific language Paul declares that we shall still be whole persons, each still a complete *nephesh*, a new creation.

He did not think up this idea himself, he found it all there already in "Moses and all the prophets". Moreover, he could do no other as he was faced with the fact of the 'once-for-all-ness' of Jesus, the Centre. Even in this life we are not naked souls clothed in dispensable bodies. We are aware that each of us becomes marked and changed as we bear on our whole *nephesh* the imprint of our social relationships. We grow in spirit as we grow in stature even as we learn to be obedient to parents, and in turn to teach our children likewise. Hebrew life and education was geared to this objective, to becoming mature in spirit. However, to understand this as continuing after death required the idea of resurrection, since death is a real terminus of the whole person.

And this is precisely what we have with Jesus, in spite of the reality of death - resurrection, the restoration to life of the dead, and so he told the disciples in John 14:2, "I go to prepare a place for you". This promise reveals that beyond death we shall receive 'bodily space'. In this life we already know that we need such just to be human beings. "In my Father's house", Jesus explains, "there is ample room for everyone's special 'space'". The space that we know here in our bodily flesh, which is all bound up with our human relationships and our physical environment, will still be there in heaven.

The word 'heaven' is of course a symbol. As the physical heavens were higher than the earth, they became a symbol for our future state, and many human languages use the same word for the sky as for heaven.

All this, as we have noted, is wholly dependent upon the reality of the resurrected Jesus. His disciples did not meet with the 'immortal soul' of Jesus, they met with Jesus. They did not meet with his ghost, far less a vision of a mere philosophical or theological concept. They

met with Jesus. He revealed to them who he was when he invited them
to recognise his identity with the crucified one of only a few days
previously; "Look at my hands and my feet... put your finger in the
wound in my side" (Luke 24:36-40; John 20:25). Thereby he was
establishing the continuity (the 'oneness') of God's redemptive purpose,
right through pain and rejection from the historical event of the
crucifixion in Jerusalem, through death itself to resurrection.

The disciples, then, met with the risen Christ whom they had
known as the crucified one. But he too had never been a naked soul.
As an embryo in his mother's womb it was her blood that flowed
through his growing veins. As a child, through his bodily conditioned
ears, eyes and 'heart' he had learned to be part of family life. At the
age when a Jewish boy becomes a *Bar-Mitzvah*, he both learned and
adopted into himself the teaching of the Temple priests. "Although he
was a Son, he learned obedience through what he suffered" (Hebrews
5:8). So the Jesus whom they encountered was the whole, complete,
'perfect' Jesus, not a mere soul but he who "became the source of
eternal salvation for all who obey him" (v.9). It is then this Jesus who,
by grace, bestows now upon us his loved ones his own fullness of life
and love through the forgiveness of our sins, the forgiveness that is of
the Holy Trinity, the eternal Creator God the Saviour.

We can never neglect the mystery of the reality of the God-head.
"Jesus rose from the dead", we read, for he as Son of God was the Lord
of both death and hell. "God raised him from the dead", we also read,
for as Son of Man he was subject to the power of death. The mystery
of the Resurrection reminds us it would be both stupid and blasphemous
of us to ask which of the two, both actually Biblical statements, was
the true one.

We have already seen that the birth of the baby Jesus is regarded
as the first-fruits of the new creation of a new humanity; there had
been of course, the "old Adam", whom we learn about in Genesis, but
here now is the new Adam (the new *ha-adam*, the new humanity) in
person. So we must go back to the early chapters of Genesis to see the
connection.

Both the man Adam and the woman Eve have their origin from
God. It is not described in modern scientific language - were it so, the
Bible's account of creation could not possibly communicate to every
generation and culture as it does. Both are born of the Word of God
together as one unity (Genesis 1:27). Later they are differentiated,
representing the actual fact of there being two genders in humanity.
"The Lord God caused a deep sleep to fall upon the man [the Hebrew
word for sleep here does not mean the sleep we enjoy each night but
suggests a supernatural event] and he slept; then he took one of his ribs
and closed up its place with flesh" (Genesis 2:21).

We should note that this word for rib is not the usual medical term that we employ. It occurs elsewhere e.g. at 1 Kings 6:34, where it means the one leaf of a double door. So instead of 'rib' for the Hebrew word *tsela'*, which can also mean the side of a mountain, or the wing of a building, or a plank of wood, we might have here a picture of a whole half of a human being who had first been fashioned like two equal folding doors. In other words, the male and female are totally equal - though they may reveal different carvings on their surfaces from each other - and are mutually necessary partners. In his wisdom God sub-divided *ha-adam*, not just 'Mr Adam', into two equal parts so that together with the Holy Spirit (as we shall see later) they may echo on earth the joyous, loving, creative fellowship of the triune God.

This new 'dual' creation of man and wife create offspring in their turn. Now we are coming down from the heights of theological myth to the earth we know. Genesis 4:1 runs: "Now the man, Adam, knew his wife, Eve, and she conceived and bore Cain". "Knew" refers to what our legal systems call 'carnal knowledge'; then the words "conceived and bore" are verbs we also use to describe the natural process of bringing a child into the world. The verse then continues with Eve saying: "I have produced a man with the help of the Lord".

"Produced" is actually 'cained', and is a Hebrew pun upon the name of their baby which we shall look at. Evidently she had become aware that human birth is not merely a physical phenomenon, but also (on the other side of the coin) *eth Yahweh*. *Eth* may be one of two different words spelt alike. One of the two is used in Hebrew as a pointer to the fact that the noun it precedes is definite and no mere abstraction. Thus, as used here, it might mean: "I have produced a man - and he is the Lord!". The other meaning of *eth* is the simple word 'with'; in which case the English versions agree to render it by "with [the help of] the Lord". However, *eth* is not a very common word for 'with', probably because it can be easily confused with the more common first meaning we have looked at. In its place the everyday word for 'with' (*'im*), would be much more likely to have been chosen.

What have we here then in typical Hebrew terms is a little word which may well be conveying both these possible English meanings at once. Thus what is both at once a historical and a theological exposition of this birth event, that is of the first human creation, is telling us in picture language that procreation began as a divine-human event. Never again do we meet with this exciting phraseology, not even in the very next verse, "next she bore his brother Abel". Evidently we are meant to learn that the old Adam originated by the action of God and man to become spirit and flesh, body and soul, one *nephesh*. The offspring of Adam, while generated from the flesh of Adam by intercourse, are at the same time brought into being by God.

But Jesus is the New Adam. The first son of Adam was born *eth Yahweh* in a deeply theological sense both of God and of sinful humanity together. Must not the baby Jesus, the New Adam, have been born likewise, both of God's Holy Spirit, and of sinful humanity at once? Indeed, but with this difference. His mother, Mary, was living the 'mysterious' life of the forgiven sinner that showed itself in her total commitment to the will of God. This she had learned and received from the revelation of himself as Saviour that God had given to Israel throughout her whole long story (Luke 1:38). I employ here this term whose root is *pele'* that occurs in Genesis 18:14. There Sarah's strange visitor promises her a child in her old age using the words "is anything too wonderful, mysterious, extra-ordinary, for the LORD?" If this is true of Christ's birth should it not also be true of his resurrection to be with God for ever?

Jesus believed so, for his last words from the Cross before his death were, "Father, into your hands I commend my spirit" (Luke 23:46). Jesus was declaring that since God is the same yesterday, today and forever, eternally the same, the living God, then God, his Father, would act in the same way to establish him in his resurrection, as had been true of his birth from the womb of Mary. He could quote the words of Isaiah 43:11 (whose name means, we recall, the Lord is Saviour): "I am the LORD and besides me there is no saviour... my salvation will be forever and my deliverance will never be ended" - even when human beings, just as happens with gnats, must meet their natural end. But as God is love and has, from the beginning, been Saviour of mankind, and since God does not change, he must continue to be the Saviour, not only of the living but also of the dead. This means that the dead are still there for him to love and redeem. We recall how Jesus rebuked the un-faith of a group of Sadducees about the state of the dead. "You know neither the Scriptures nor the power of God. Have you not read in the Book of Moses, in the story about the bush [Exodus 3], how God said to him, 'I am the God of Abraham, the God of Isaac and the God of Jacob' [note, each person is named separately and not herded together as a mere group in history]. He is not the God of the dead, but of the living; you are quite wrong'[!]" (Mark 12:24-27).

Accordingly, then, we turn and look at what Christ understood death to be. In the days of his flesh he assured a gathering of simple, believing people about a little girl of twelve, "She is not dead, but asleep" (Matthew 9:24). Jesus was employing the language we have looked at already, that sleep must precede the entry into the new creation (Genesis 2:21), in this case the fullness of life God offers us in

Christ. Real death, whatever that may mean, on the other hand, can take place in a person's life here and now, if they have refused the forgiveness, love and care of the Lord of Life. Jesus pointed to just such a reality when a young man, whom Jesus must have known along with his family members, requested permission not to accompany Jesus straight away (Matthew 8:21-22), in order to attend his father's funeral. Whereupon Jesus replied: "Follow me, and let the dead bury their dead". In the meantime, we might add, Jesus reminded him that his turn to 'die' must eventually come, but, as with the first creation, the new creation too must be preceded by a sleep. So it would be with this young man; he was to become, in Christ, a member of the new creation in heaven, for he would share in Christ's mysterious, extraordinary, *pele'*, transition from death to life. In the words of Handel's *Messiah* we sing, "And we shall be changed" (2 Corinthians 3:18 KJV); but with today's vocabulary we prefer the verb 'transfigured'. It is quite un-Hebraic to conclude that that 'sleep' is a sleep of the ages, that the dead in Christ must endure what some would call 'soul sleep' that will last for millennia until the sounding of the 'last trumpet', to be followed by the Last Judgement. Another aspect of such 'sleep' has been the doctrine of the existence of a state known as Limbo, though, with the recovery of biblical theology in this generation, it has been largely abandoned. 'Soul sleep' implies a Platonic universe. From our side, there is a time-lag before resurrection. But from God's side, we go immediately to heaven.

Jesus taught in parables. Parables do not record scientific fact, rather they convey truth in pictures. How does Jesus picture the Last Judgement for us? We look at Matthew 25:31-46. There Jesus gives us an eschatological picture of judgement; we know this is so at once for he 'immediately' paints a picture of the eternal significance of himself surrounded in glory by all the host of angels. But he keeps our minds firmly at the level of earth and of the behaviour of ordinary human persons; human beings are not angels. He reminds us of this since he chooses to describe himself here by the title he gives himself, Son of Man.

Paul, with his eye on this parable of Jesus, insisted that, "Now is the judgement of the world, now is the day of salvation". Feeding the hungry, clothing the naked, caring for the sick, these all, in the light of the presence of the Galilean Son of Man, have received already, here and now, the judgement "Yes". Their actions are therefore eschatologically meaningful. Those who, on the streets of Nazareth or Jerusalem, did not clothe the naked, or love their neighbour as their own self (meaning, remember, that the neighbour needs their love as they hope the neighbour will love them) have already 'shouted without words' God's judgement of "No", so loudly that it can be heard in eternity.

Again we see the Hebraic belief in the mystery of 'one'. God is one, creation is one, time and eternity are one. A word spoken in Capernaum or New York can be heard at "the throne of His glory" (v31). But more crucially Jesus' parable shows us that God judges us when walking the road alongside of us and not from a throne in the sky, so that in consequence he feels the pains in his own 'heart' of our selfishness, greed and cruelty.

This is not to say we should abandon the concept of a Last Judgement, rather, we are to take Jesus seriously when he speaks of the serious business of human behaviour here and now. He reminds us that every decision we take, to love or not to love, is the very last judgement we shall ever make in the case of each new human relationship we encounter, for it is a *fait accompli*; and so serious that it will have its ultimate outcome at the end of time.

This relationship between time and eternity has been revealed to us in the person of Christ incarnate. In his Galilee days it took time for Jesus to grow up, from infancy to manhood, as it also took time for him to learn God's will for himself always each new day. This was true for him right till his last day when, in the Garden of Gethsemane he still had something to learn of the will of God for him. Now, of course, as the risen Christ, he was still the same *nephesh* developed in time, for time had become woven into the growth of his physical body and into the development of his commitment and obedience.

Time itself has to share in redemption. Thus it was that our 'developed-by-time' Jesus carried into the 'timeless' Godhead, not just the mortal 'time' of Jesus of Nazareth, but its *aharith*, its eschatological significance, its time made real for ever in the Resurrection. In the Person of the resurrected Christ the effect of created time had now been brought within and into the 'experience' of the eternal Godhead. The Person of Christ had introduced in himself the first-fruits of the new cosmos, although these had been enjoyed by God himself since the beginning, for "on the seventh day" (Genesis 2:1-3) "God rested" in deep satisfaction in the knowledge that his employment of matter, space and time was very good. Now however there was carried into the Godhead the enjoyment of creation from within it, and that was "the perfect rest of the people of God".

Contrary-wise, eternity itself can now, at our human level of understanding, be conceived as a variable. We, subject to time, can look back upon the reality, before the Incarnation, that "God was in Israel". Moreover, it is the Resurrection of Christ that has interpreted for us how such a statement as we have at Genesis 6:6 could have any validity for us: "And the LORD was sorry he had made humankind on the earth, and it grieved him to his heart". The Hebrew verb *niham* has to be understood in terms of an actual change in the mind of God. It needs to be translated by several different English verbs, by 'be moved to pity', 'have compassion', 'suffer grief', 'repent' in the sense of changing one's plan - but all with an awareness of the costliness to God of what he sees he must do. If "God was in Christ" (2 Corinthians 5:19) reconciling the cosmos to himself (note - not just humanity, nor just this planet Earth, but the whole universe), then God himself, in the human person of Jesus, had descended into death and had entered the hell of the chaos that had been God's arch enemy ever since the beginning (Genesis 1:2). Thus, as 'Son of Man' Jesus really died, gripped, pressed and held down in terms of time - three days - inert in the power of the evil one. But as 'Son of the Living God' he arose from the grave to be the first fruits of the new creation. As such he was Paul's *arrabon* (2 Corinthians 1:22; Ephesians 1:14), the pledge, the down-payment, the first instalment towards the final establishment of "the Kingdom of God" that Jesus, Son of Man, had inaugurated by his Incarnation.

But more, as Son of Man, Jesus needed not just time to grow "in favour with God and man" (Luke 2:52), he also needed food, food that grew out of the soil. In other words his physical structure was gradually being reconstructed and sustained from elements of his physical environment. These elements had necessarily become integrated into his whole *nephesh*; this fact the disciples could see for themselves when he appeared to them in the Upper Room, the very room where only days before he had eaten food with them. We are thus left with the inference that Jesus in his Person was now the first-fruits of the new nature, the new cosmos, and as well as being such, victor over the powers of evil. There had always been the promise of the redemption of nature, when, for example, the lion would lie down with the lamb; but God's total plan of salvation included the Holy Land, the very soil that had now fed the Son of Man. As Paul put it at Romans 8:22ff, "We know that the whole creation has been groaning in labor pains till now; and not only the creation, but we ourselves, who have the first fruits of the Spirit..." - "and of the new heaven and the new earth, wherein dwells righteousness". This promise had now been fulfilled in the Person of the resurrected Christ.

(See my chapter, "Israel - the Land and the Resurrection" in *The Witness of the Jews to God*, p.32.)

Chapter Six

THE CHURCH

The human race (the 'old Adam'), as we have seen, was born out of what is physical by the Spirit (Genesis 4:2). So it was in the case of the birth of the 'new Adam', as Paul calls Christ, he too was born in the flesh by the Spirit (Matthew 1:18). So what of the church? Just what we would expect. At Pentecost it too was born again in the flesh by the Spirit (Acts 2:1-4).

The social sciences regard the Church as a sociological phenomenon. It undoubtedly is such. But if we dare to think Hebraically we discover that this 'sociological phenomenon' is only one side of the coin. The other side reveals it as a 'theological phenomenon' as well. Since it is such, each of the two sides can be the object of our study, separately, whereupon we discover that it is as truly of God as it is of the human race. The two together mean that where the Church is physical it is born by the Spirit, existing now by lasting into eternity.

We are inclined to read into the New Testament the idea that the Church was 'born' at Pentecost. Not so: rather we read in Acts 1 and 2 how it was Israelites now living in *diaspora* on whom the Spirit fell - the chosen people of old to whom the prophet Joel had promised the outpouring of the Spirit (Joel 2:28-29). They were even identified here by the Hebrew term for 'church', viz *qahal*. At Pentecost, therefore, it would be more correct to say that the Church was 'reborn', for it had actually come into being long before in response to God's promise to Abraham (Genesis 12:1-3).

It began of God. God, the all-wise, the all-knowing, the Creator of both time and eternity, at his own chosen moment in the history of his planet Earth, uttered his Word to a Mesopotamian shepherd. He said just the one word "Go!" (Genesis 12:1). The speaker was the LORD, the recipient was a human creature, not a robot but one of *ha-adam*, made in the image of God. He was - and this is highly important - a person, a *nephesh*, whose experience was marked by both self-understanding and free-will. He was called in his 'heart' to go into the unknown, to a 'place' unknown, to reach it at a time unknown, and yet (as only later generations could recognise) for a purpose that was known to God; and though this Word was uttered at an unknown yet specific moment to 'Father Abraham', yet in time it was worked out in the life and experience of Abraham, and of his descendants, accomplishing all it had promised.

Abraham could have said, "No", as a self-centred, sinful human being is free to do. But by grace in his heart he said, "Yes", and held to it even when he went on to learn the terms of his election and of his mission. He was to make a clean break from his family, his culture, his learning, his language, his Mesopotamian gods, for from him (as the narrator tells us) was to stem a new sociological phenomenon - a great nation.

As we read on in the story (Genesis 12ff.) we are almost shocked to discover that, humanly speaking, God's promise cannot possibly come true; for Abraham's wife, Sarah, was already an old lady, too late in life to bear a child. However, to meet this *contretemps* we are told of two factors, one, on the human level, being Abraham's constant faith and commitment, which the narrator tells us was counted to him as being "in the right with God". This factor remained constant: at each stage of his journey into the unknown of both place and time he erected an altar to the LORD, and then moved on.

The other factor, which we have already referred to in a previous chapter, was the incident when a strange visitor encouraged the old couple by asking them to remember that with God all things are possible, in the words "Is anything too hard [*pele'*, mysterious, supernaturally different, impossible] for the LORD?" A child was thus born "of the LORD", and God's promise was actualised. From this child were born in turn all who bore the name of Israel.

The Israelite people had thus been born by grace; had been sustained throughout every conceivable vicissitude of human stupidity, disgrace, lust, rebellion and even "hardening of their heart" against this divine grace (cf. Psalm 95). Yet it was this people with whom God chose to make his covenant of love, the content of which was the unshakeable, loyal, creative, compassionate, suffering love of God (all of these adjectives are needed to explain the Hebrew term *hesed*). This content, as the eminent Old Testament scholar H.Wheeler Robinson put it fifty years ago, is like the life-giving milk that belongs in and is the content of the unbreakable hard nut of a coconut shell. The latter is the eternal covenant itself. It was by grace that God put it in the mouth of the great prophet of the Exile in Babylon to say to his miserable people: "I have put my words in your mouth, and hidden you in the shadow of my hand; even as I was stretching out the heavens and laying the foundation of the earth, I was saying to Zion, 'You are my people'". Even at that time it seems, all was of grace (Isaiah 51:16).

As a 'sociological phenomenon' this people were given a human framework. In tune with the sociological construction of the nations in the second millennium before Christ, they were constituted in the patriarchal form of twelve tribes, each of them named from one of the descendants of Abraham and Isaac. We are not to deride the ensuing structure of the Israelite nation, living as we do in a totally different social, economic and political world.

It is interesting to note that two numbers were adopted and adhered to to regulate the human element in this new creation, the People of God. These were the number 70 (the strange multiple of the mystic basic number 7, which all the peoples of the Near East held to as a vital unit of time) and the number 7 itself; the latter contained within it that other mystery, the Sabbath day, the rest day of God himself (Genesis 2:2).

Genesis 10 lists all the peoples of the then known world, 70 nations in all. But Israel's name is not amongst them! The reason for this is to put in perspective and signify the reality of Israel's mission to all humankind. That was what the Covenant was all about. At its institution (Exodus 19:5-6) this is what Moses declared to Israel from God:

> Thus you shall say to the house of Jacob, and tell the Israelites: "You have seen what I did to the Egyptians, and how I bore you on eagles' wings and brought you to myself. Now therefore, if you obey my voice and keep my covenant, you shall be my treasured possession out of all the peoples. Indeed, the whole earth is mine, but you shall be for me a priestly kingdom and a holy nation." These are the words that you shall speak to the Israelites.

It was Second Isaiah, the Prophet of the Exile, whom we have newly quoted, who reminded his people that the Covenant still stood even in exile, and that they were still one whole priestly kingdom (under the one God, the King of creation). His words were:

> It is too light a thing [too easy, almost superficial] that you should be my servant to raise up the tribes of Jacob [scattered and disheartened in Babylon] and to restore the survivors of Israel; I will give you as a light to the nations, that my salvation may reach [in your very persons] to the end of the earth.

This 'oneness', this 'wholeness' of the one God's relations with his chosen people, keeps cropping up. He had chosen them as one unit, though they were under the indictment that as a whole they had rebelled against his plan and purpose for them; consequently they were all, as one whole, under the judgement of God, the good, the bad,

the indifferent, babies and all! (See Psalm 137:7-9). That was to be
God's final judgement, pictured for us in the parable story of Noah
and the Flood. But, as we have learned from the Song of Moses
(Deuteronomy 32), steadfast love, *hesed*, and compassion lie behind
God's justice and judgement; we learn in fact, that his justice and
recompense reveal themselves as his own activity when by means of
one total act, "He died for all", as the New Testament expresses it. In
consequence all the people of God can now exclaim, "We are
forgiven", even before we repent. No wonder then that Second Isaiah
(43:21), can go on to refer to "the people whom I formed for myself,
that they might declare my praise".

Has all this, then, any relevance for the church of the New
Testament? Straight away we are to note that the Church is never
known as the New Israel. There is only one Israel, and it remains to
this day as the divine community of the Jewish people. In Romans 11
Paul deals with this issue at length. On the other hand the prophets
Isaiah, Jeremiah, Micah and others looked forward to the day when
"a remnant shall *shubb*", 'right-about-turn', and come back home to
God, leaving behind them all their foolish ways. Paul refers to it in
Romans 11:5 in that same passage. It is through this Remnant,
moreover, (the term employed by the great prophets), that the key
note of 'incarnation' is maintained. It must necessarily be so, since the
one-ness of God becomes the one-ness of his work through incarnation
at all periods of his plan of redemption. It is possible for us to be struck
by the idea that in the death of Christ we witness the end of
incarnation. But incarnation was actually now only entering upon a
new phase. Moments before the risen Christ's 'Ascension' he had this
to say to his disciples: "You will receive power when the Holy Spirit
has come upon you" (Acts 1:6-11). "When he had said this, as they
were watching, he was lifted up, and a cloud took him out of their
sight". It would be all wrong for us in the space age merely to pour
scorn upon the naïvety of the biblical narrative. The disciples would
instead have a mental vision of the 'rapture' of the great prophet
Elijah, when "the Lord took Elijah up to heaven by a whirlwind" (2
Kings 2:1), a story which all Israel knew had a theological rather than
a factual content. And so "a cloud took him out of their sight". As
good Hebraists they recalled that when Moses ascended up Mount
Sinai to speak with God, "who dwells within the cloud", beyond
human sight and philosophy, Moses had to disappear from Israel's
sight in his turn within the cloud. All this is, of course, parabolic
theological language.

The theological picture continues: "Suddenly two men in white
stood by them". We recall that angels everywhere are envisioned as
incarnations in human form, and that 'white' speaks to us of the

purity and holiness of God when his 'glory' is seen in our human experience. Then follows the important announcement of the continuity of the incarnate Word: "This Jesus, who has been taken up from you into heaven, will come in the same way as you saw him go into heaven". Not, we may be assured, by some divine parachute, but in some sense as Moses reappeared to Israel when he "came down out of a dense cloud" (Exodus 19:9), accompanied by "thunder and lightning, as well as a thick cloud on the mountain" (v.16). "Let neither the priests nor the people break through to come up to the LORD; otherwise he will break out against them" (v.24). Clearly humankind must not try literally to follow Christ in approaching the realm of the Spirit, thereby neglecting the Incarnation which is our bond to the Lord our God. "It is not for you to know the times or periods..." said the risen Christ to his faithful - but all too curious - followers before his Ascension to the Father. Apocalyptic writing, as in the New Testament book of Revelation, is not given us to be a humanly discernible map of things to come.

Then there was a short pause in events, during which time Peter was the only one able to adjust the thinking and understanding of "the believers - together these numbered about one hundred and twenty persons" (Acts 1:15), by expounding how "the Scripture had to be fulfilled".

Then it happened, on the day of Pentecost (cf. Numbers 11:24-30). It was revealed that Christ was alive, "although **you** killed the Prince of life" (REV). He had been killed, God had raised him up, having freed him from death, and he was now exalted at the right hand of God, "having received from the Father the promise of the Spirit": "This he has poured out, as you both see and hear", "all of them were filled with the Holy Spirit". Thus just as God had once breathed physical breath into *ha-adam*'s nostrils (Genesis 2:7), so now in an even more intimate way, God poured out his Spirit into the whole *nephesh* of man, in a new way and for a new purpose. But this time it was with God's chosen 'man', Israel as a whole, in order that Israel might be a "light to lighten the Gentiles", with the purpose that "my salvation may reach to the end of the earth" (Isaiah 49:6); this 'remnant of Israel' was being empowered (and the term 'power' is emphasised by the pictorial language here) to be, in action not just talk, the human instrument that could and must now witness to God's loving purpose. This human instrument was a collection of peoples gathered in one place in Jerusalem from out of the whole list of countries that are named in this passage of Acts.

All of them were Jews, yet very probably having with them proselytes, 'enquirers', who were asking to join God's people Israel. All of these were members of the *diaspora* living amongst the 70 nations of the earth (Genesis 10). At the Pentecost event the wind and the tongues of fire (note, the text says "as of fire" - we are in the realm of theology expressed in parable) "filled the entire house where they were sitting", where in other words they all underwent a communal experience. But then next we read: "A tongue rested upon each of them"; the grace of God's empowerment showed no distinction of individual persons - some were Parthian Jews, others were from Judea, the historical root of God's chosen people.

We should note that the Pentecost experience illustrated exactly what Jesus had promised his disciples: "In my Father's house there are many mansions" (KJV) - 'rooms' in modern versions. The Church, both here and 'above' is one community, since Israel as a whole has always been the people of God. But individuals are never 'lost in the crowd', as we might put it today; each has his/her own 'room' to be a private individual, or again to put it in today's jargon, are given the 'space' we need to be the kind of people God intends us to be (Matthew 6:6). So, to go back to Paul's imagery of the Church, both here and 'above', the Church is the Body of Christ, but each single believer is like a limb of the body, even a finger, separate and independent, yet wholly dependent upon its relationship to the Body (1 Corinthians 12:12-27).

The New Testament remains faithful to the revelation of the unity of God that is displayed throughout the whole of the Old Testament. As that unity can only be interpreted to us by means of metaphors, so we find that the New Testament too makes full use of human metaphors to describe this unique phenomenon in the human story, the church. We saw in an earlier chapter that Israel could regard herself as a corporate personality. In that chapter we noted, for example, how all Israel, as one entity, could request the Moabite people to "let me pass through thy land". John Wesley, in his turn, three centuries ago made it clear that there is no such thing as an individual Christian. "The Church", he said, "following Paul's teaching, being the Body, individuals are thereby limbs (Latin, 'members') that owe their life to being nourished by the blood from the whole Body". Each metaphor the New Testament employs shows this dual-nature-in-one characteristic - following the Incarnation itself.

And even within the comprehensive duality that incarnation implies, the one-ness of God and of his creative plan employ twin metaphors (like the coin) to further interpret this great theme of the Bible. We have seen that the Church is revealed to be one Body, one unit, in God's purpose and plan. But within the Body the individual believer too is both in and of the Body, and so he/she is now an individual child of God. This metaphor, then, 'child of God', reveals to us the significance of Jeremiah's experience as he heard the Word addressed to him: "Before I formed you in the womb I knew you, and before you were born I consecrated you" (Jeremiah 1:5). "Whose womb was it?" we ask, remembering also that the verb 'to know' can occur as a metaphorical substitute for 'carnal knowledge'. Was Jeremiah's mother not representing Mother Israel, and was Jeremiah's Father not he who chose him before the foundation of the world? (cf. Ephesians 1:4)

John 19:25-27 runs:

> Meanwhile, standing near the cross of Jesus were his mother, and his mother's sister, Mary the wife of Clopas and Mary Magdalene. When Jesus saw his mother and the disciple whom he loved standing beside her, he said to his mother, "Woman, here is your son." Then he said to the disciple, "Here is your mother". And from that hour the disciple took her into his own home.

In his *Mary for All Christians* (p.205 - the book depends on J.Patsch, *Maria, die Mutter des Herrn*, Benziger Verlag, 1953), John Macquarrie writes:

> Under the cross, John is not simply a private individual, he is also an apostle, a foundation-stone and a representative of the Church. What the Master says to him, he says to the whole Church.

Consequently Macquarrie can then comment: "The idea is already there that Mary, the mother of Jesus, is also the mother of the Church which is his body."

One of the most Hebraically minded of the early Church Fathers, Cyprian, living around 250 CE, was the one who denounced the strong dualistic heretical groups of his day. Cyprian made this telling epigrammatical claim: "No man can call God 'Father' who does not call the Church 'Mother'".

Moreover Cyprian taught this theological truth in practice. As bishop of Carthage in North Africa he raised a massive sum of money to ransom thousands of his own people after plague and barbarian raiders in 252-253 CE had decimated his province and diocese. The Church had stood firm throughout. "No wonder schismatics were reconciled and converts came in in droves. Cyprian speaks of the 'new population of believers'" (W.H.C. Frend, *The Rise of Christianity*, p.324). He was aware that the task of ancient Israel was to be just that, the mother of the nations of mankind. To this Old Testament summons to Israel Jesus added: "The works that the Father has given me to complete, the very works that I am doing (see end of chapter 5), testify on my behalf that the Father has sent me" (John 5:36). "Believe me because of the works themselves" (John 14:11). And now, the

Holy Spirit, he whom Christ had said "the Father will send in my name" (John 14:26), was guiding the Church, the 'extension' of the Incarnation, to do the same works of motherly care and compassion. Since this is what motherhood means in terms of the Incarnation, some of the keen feminist theologians of today, ask us to address God either as Mother, or as Father-Mother; but are thereby unwittingly more nearly Neo-Platonists than Hebraists.

We turn for help in this matter to Jesus himself. At that solemn moment when, with his disciples, he celebrated the Passover Supper in the Upper Room, we read that Jesus took bread, broke it, and gave it to his disciples, saying, "This is my Body, broken for you". It was then that he cited a highlight in the preaching of the prophet Jeremiah (31:31-34), quoted in turn for our sakes by Paul at 1 Corinthians 11:23-26. Jeremiah's passage deals with a promise by God that he would make a new covenant with all the People of God. This was despite the fact that they had been unfaithful to the covenant, although he had "taken them by the hand" and then ratified it with them in Moses' day. "This covenant they broke, though I was their husband, says the LORD". Two realities are intertwined here - marriage and covenant making. We shall look at each in turn.

First the term 'husband'. We must be careful, for in the Hebrew of the Old Testament there are two words for husband; there is *'ish*, and there is *ba'al* (which actually means more 'master').

It is not surprising to find that when Jeremiah was hustled off against his will into exile in Egypt in 587 BCE he was shocked to find there a shrine, perhaps even a temple, built to honour *Yahweh*'s spouse, the Queen of Heaven. She was of course a concept taken from the Canaanite goddess *Ashera*, as she occurs in Hebrew, originally the bloody wife of the *Ba'al* of the Canaanites.

Hosea was the first Old Testament prophet to distinguish between the two terms *'ish* and *ba'al*. The latter is actually the name of this god of the Canaanites, the god of nature, including the products of nature, grain, wine and oil (Hosea 2:8 REB). Yet *Yahweh*'s love and grace actually induces Israel to say to him, "You are my *'ish*, and no longer will I call you my *ba'al*". For *ba'al* was quite a common title for *Yahweh* before Hosea's day (See my writings, *From Moses to Paul: A Christological Study in the Light of our Hebraic Heritage*, and, *A Biblical Approach to the Doctrine of the Trinity*, p.45). It was also employed for the head of the 'psychic community' within Israel (*ibid.*, p. 36). This definition is expressed in a revelatory picture in the Song of Songs some centuries later. The collection of poems there begins by referring to Solomon and his harem, where he is seen as the *ba'al* of scores of wives and concubines. In contrast with Solomon the young couple who are so deeply in love with each other illustrate for us how God is in fact the *'ish* of Israel, her one and only true husband, and not her *ba'al*, in that the couple are bound together by a love that death cannot touch. (See my commentary on the Song of Songs, *Revelation of God*.)

We may look at the language employed for husband especially as we meet it in Deutero-Isaiah, but always with a side look at Hosea. We begin with Isaiah 54:5, "Realise that [*ki*] your Maker ['*osaikh*, in the feminine plural, because 'God' in Hebrew is *'elohim*, plural] is your husband" [and so *ba'al* follows also in the feminine plural, *bo'alaikh*]. Yet the very next word is "*Yahweh*", defined in the singular as "Lord of hosts", and as "the Holy One of Israel", your redeemer, *go'el*. This *Yahweh* once redeemed you by rescuing you from Egypt; he brought you into covenant with himself, making you one with himself, even as a wife is one with her husband. Despite the fact that *Yahweh* is seen as absolutely holy, he is pictured as marrying the whore Israel! "For the Lord has called you", the text continues, "he chose you, he invited you [feminine] and you alone to 'consort' with him. He found you as an *'ishsha* [v.6, the feminine form of *'ish*] when you were forsaken and grieved in spirit. This calling you was an act of grace alone, for it included the forgiveness of the "fornications of your youth". (See H.D. Beeby's commentary on Hosea, *Grace Abounding*, p.30.)

In other words Yahweh had married her in order to redeem her. As Paul declares, it is possible for a woman or a man to be 'redeemed' through the faith and love of the spouse. In the case of the Old Testament, Israel is redeemed by the *hesed*, the steadfast love of the marriage covenant.

This marriage had rescued her from slavery (to her instincts and ideologies, could we say?); it was made with her that she might possess the *shalom* - fullness of life and peace - which comes from the covenant; it demonstrated *Yahweh*'s total forgiveness of Israel's youthful excesses. It let her forget the past and think only of the life lying before them both of shared grace. And since God does not change, but is the same yesterday, today and for ever, to enter into this marriage was to enter into a life of love that must ultimately continue through death into eternity.

The relationship between God and his people has never ceased. As Third Isaiah rejoiced to declare, and thrillingly acknowledged: his own people, now rescued and redeemed from the 'hell' of Babylon, were the living promise of the great redemptive act still to come: "For as a young man marries a young woman, and as the Bridegroom rejoices over the bride, so shall your God rejoice over you" (Isaiah 62:5).

This then is how Jeremiah connects the word for 'husband' with the promise of a new covenant to be gained through the marriage relationship. This relationship had already been expressed by Hosea in terms of eschatological promise (Hosea 2:16-23). Hosea actually prefaces the promise with the words *ne'um Yahweh*, not the usual "says the Lord". These two words mean much more than 'say'. 'Decisive declaration' is one scholar's suggestion, in other words something that is absolute. The whole action of God is one of grace alone. Israel will no longer address God by the term *ba'al*, master, reserving that title for the gods of nature. Yahweh will be her *'ish*, her monogamous husband, and the relationship will be *le 'olam*, to all eternity, once it comes to pass "on that day"; and the relationship will embrace even the beasts and the birds, as well as all snakes and nature red in tooth and claw. So, included in the covenant is the grain, the wine, and the oil that Israel had thought to be the province of the god *Ba'al*. Moreover the content of the new covenant was to be in terms of justice, righteousness, steadfast love, *hesed* and mercy (the Hebrew word used for a woman's almost physical compassion for the child of her womb). For, as Hosea 2:19-20 declares, all that is mentioned in vv.21-23 is to be included in the new betrothal, and all linked with the reality that Israel "will know the Lord" (*yada'*, the same word for know as is used in Genesis 4:1).

No wonder, by the way, that Christian marriage is in our day distinguished forcibly from mere legal marriage when, in dependence upon Hosea, both partners employ the active verb in making their promise: "I covenant... [in total loyalty, *hesed*] ...till death do us part". In fact the popular way of interpreting the term 'eschatological' is simply to say that marriages are made in heaven. Moreover, we are to remember that included in this covenanting is the declaration "with my body I thee worship".

We read that the old priest Simeon (Luke 2:25), steeped as he was in the affirmations of the Prophets, "the Holy Spirit being upon him, was looking for the 'consolation' of Israel"; he was looking for the divine Husband to take his Virgin Bride in his arms and in compassionate love 'console' her by 'consummating' their covenantal marriage together. And God actually did so when the Holy Spirit incarnated the Word in the womb of Mary, and God became a human in the person of Christ. The union of God and humankind in the Christ is thus the final fulfilment of God's marriage to Israel, and through them to all humankind in the person of Christ.

Mary is sometimes referred to as 'the Mother of God', but is also seen as the Mother of the people of God, the Church, since she herself participates in the salvation of her Son; and as the first to acknowledge the grace of God in him, is seen as the prototype of all who believe.

We return to Jeremiah 31:32, but find, curiously enough, that Jeremiah used for the idea of husband, not the noun *ba'al*, but the verb of the same root. What we have here is the form "to *ba'al* them". The verse runs: "my covenant which they broke when I took them by the hand to bring them out of the land of Egypt... though [very emphatic] I had *ba'al*ed them", using the preposition *b* after the verb.

First, we should note that the various versions do not like this verb at all. The Septuagint (Jeremiah 38:32) has *emelesa auton*, "I disregarded them", instead of the Hebrew *ba'al*. It is followed likewise by the Vulgate. We should not forget that these are two texts used by the early Church Fathers as they wrestled to produce the western orthodoxy that we have inherited today. Then, second, the New Covenant, in the thought of the prophets from Hosea onwards (and Jeremiah has clearly soaked himself in Hosea's material) implies that Yahweh is to be known to Israel as *'ish*, her monogamous and only true Husband. For *'ish* occurs five times oftener than *ba'al* in the Old Testament to describe even a human husband. Yet Jeremiah uses the verb *ba'al* twice in this passage. So we must suppose that he is expressing the idea first of all, not of marriage, but of taking in marriage, or of marrying. And since both times the verb is reserved for God's action in choosing, even grasping hold of Israel, we are given a vivid picture of the divine activity in terms of prevenient grace. This is because, to the Hebrew ear, the verb 'to *ba'al*' has overtones of ideas such as 'to rule over', 'to own', 'to possess', 'to be lord of'. God's action in 'marrying' Israel then is to be understood in terms of the language used at Pentecost of a rushing wind sweeping his people into his arms. "Our God", says many an Old Testament passage, "is a consuming fire". Here again we discover that the 'steadfast love', the *hesed* of God, is something that has no parallel such as the religions of the old world can emulate. God's love is a jealous love, (unfortunately rendered by 'zealous' in some modern Versions). "For the LORD your God is a devouring fire, a jealous God" (Deuteronomy 4:24). He loves you passionately, you are his loved one, and he will not allow any other 'power' to snatch you out of his arms. He will not let any other god commit adultery with you. His is a jealous love, you belong to him, and you in turn must put your whole person and being in his care, and so thus trust and love him with all your heart, soul, mind and strength in return, and love no other! So, in New Testament application, Paul writes in Ephesians 5:25: "Husbands love your wives, just as Christ loved the Church, and gave himself up for her". What a command!

Paul was able to hold himself firmly to the exact words Jesus had used in what we call the Last Supper (1 Corinthians 11:23-26): "This cup is the new covenant in my blood". We must always remember that the New Testament was not written in English. Its Greek language has two words for 'new', *neos* and *kainos* (like the French *neuf* and *nouveau*). *Neos* means 'completely new', and so 'different', as a new-bought suit of clothes would be. *Kainos* means 'my good old suit I have had refurbished'. The word here at v.25 is *kainos* for the 'new covenant'. Similarly Paul speaks of the 'ancient', *palaios*, covenant, not the 'old and out-of-date one'; for God had promised he would keep his covenant for ever. By contrast Hebrew (the language of Jeremiah 31) has only one word for 'new', an adjective built from the noun *hodesh*, which is actually the name of the new moon. The good old moon rises afresh every month as 'the new moon'. And that is the exact word Jesus used to describe his new covenant. After all, in the days of his flesh, had he not declared, "I have not come to abolish, but to fulfil"? (Matthew 5:17)

So the movement around Jesus, coalescing into a 'new' community, was not an abandonment of the ancient Israelite community and the 'ancient' covenant community and the ancient covenant that had stood since Moses' day, but a new covenant community filled to the full with the *hesed*, the thrilling 'steadfast love' (Psalm 136) that God pours out upon his Church, and which he calls upon the Church to pour out, in turn, upon the world.

Throughout the Christian centuries, in consequence, theologians have recognised that we are now living in the age of the Resurrection, and of the pouring out of the Spirit by Jesus on the Church, when the Holy Spirit brings the fruit of the Incarnation into the life of the Church. What great promises Jesus made for this 'age of the Spirit'! "The one who believes in me will also do the works that I do and, in fact, will do greater works than these because I am going to the Father." (John 14:12)

While this can be interpreted purely in physical terms - the technology enabling us to eliminate infectious disease or to preach to a million people at once was, of course, unavailable even to the incarnate Christ - the context, the promise of power to the disciples, indicates that the greater works would take place as the Spirit empowered the Church, no longer localised in Galilee and limited by fear and lack of understanding. "I will ask the Father, and he will give you another Advocate, the Holy Spirit... you know him, because he abides with you, and he will be in you" (John 14:16-17). "He will teach you everything, and will remind you of all that I have said to you" (v.26).

This kind of power is indeed 'messianic'. But Jesus was unwilling himself to accept the title of 'Messiah'. For two reasons. First, his contemporaries hoped to see some kind of army general stage a coup against the Roman powers, and that was their idea of a Messiah. To squash this hope from being applied to himself, Jesus entered Jerusalem quietly on a donkey. Military dictators ride upon a white horse.

Second, and perhaps more important, Jesus hoped to show that his own people should themselves take up the task of being Messiah to the world: after all, Israel as a nation had long been known as 'son of God'. But it was not to be; instead, in the closing days of his life he foretold to his disciples, that, in the power of the Spirit it was to be the coming Church on which this task would be laid. Jesus was more than Messiah, he was LORD of all.

The Church is composed of individual persons, men, women and children. They, each and all, become 'members', limbs of the Body, by the foreordaining grace of God (cf. Jeremiah 1:5, Psalm 139:13-17). We have seen that God acted first in creating men and women to be what they are, that he acted first in bringing Israel out of Egypt and turning a gaggle of slaves into his own covenant people, that he acted first in opening the womb of Mary, the Mother of the incarnate Christ, that he acted first again at Pentecost to turn a helpless, bewildered group of deeply disappointed Diaspora Jews into the People of his choice. He did so by baptising them with his Holy Spirit.

The final instructions to his new Church by the risen Christ was to tell them by what means they were to fulfil the words of Deutero-Isaiah that Israel was to be "a light to give light to the nations of the earth"; he told them they were to "baptise all nations in the name of the Father, and of the Son, and of the Holy Spirit" (Matthew 28:19). Through the God-given love of parents, friends or congregation, by means of prayer, by means of the symbolic cleansing of water and by the inspiration of the Holy Spirit, a human being (whether baby or adult) is made a 'member' of the redeemed community, Mother Church, the People of Pentecost, the Army of the Lord. He or she receives a unique gift, one that is only for him/herself, as the object of God's prevenient grace and love in the gift of the Holy Spirit. The minister may say a prayer such as this:

> Bless this water, and fulfil your Pentecostal promise, that this child, being born again of water and the Holy Spirit, may be made part of your new creation, united for ever with Christ as a member of the Church, his Body.

This happens to be a quote from the Church of Scotland (Presbyterian) Book of Common Order, 1979. Other denominations employ virtually similar language. So God's plan to use the principle of incarnation to reveal his loving and creative self is not ended with the death of Christ. Christ receives through his Ascension the promise of the Spirit (Acts 2:33), in order to pour this Spirit out on his members. In this sense he becomes incarnate again in every person who owns his name.

Thereafter the two-way 'Hebraic' relationship between the Body and the individual member becomes apparent. The Christian individual, step by step, is 'mothered' by the Church, through

Christian education, care and guidance until such time as he or she is glad and proud to witness to Christian faith before the congregation in gratitude for his or her baptism. S/he declares that God-given and church-promoted faith which has now led him or her to seek to join in the 'mothering' call of the Church, as it faces a weary world. S/he can dare to do so, because s/he is now vividly aware of the Spirit through whom Jesus dwells incarnate in the heart and empowers us for mission.

Christian education helps us to acquire a rational and relevant faith; it reveals to us the fundamental validity of the moral life and of a true ethic that is based on love; it enables us to recognise, bit by bit, as we grow in years, that our every act for good or ill has eternal significance in the sight of God. Yet God is always our loving heavenly Father, forgiving, renewing, encouraging, enabling, till we recognise that we have been well equipped with the whole armour of God, and must now take our place, small as it may be, in the overall strategy in the Church's war against the powers of evil in all its forms, political, social, ideological, or cultural, all of them revealing misunderstandings of what it means to be human. And so, as part of the loving empowerment of the Spirit in our mortal bodies, we may throw ourselves into the fray daily, encouraged by tasting also daily the joy of the life to come.

We find we have entered into a movement that lets us participate in a long history which is of God. We learn then to believe in the stability of God, to see things as God sees them with security and 'confidence' (*emunah*, Isaiah 7:14), and find what it means to share in God's joy even as he continues to make all things new. Thus the ancient words of Isaiah 30:18 come alive: "Therefore the LORD waits to be gracious to you; therefore he will rise up to be gracious to you. Blessed are all who wait for him". Deep within this joy is the awareness of God's gift to us of being able to forgive those who have sinned against us, because, in Christ and his Cross, God has already forgiven us. The Incarnation, involving the ultimate in suffering, pain, ignominy, and rejection, is the revelation to our hearts and minds of the depths of evil and of the horrors of that self induced hell which rules the lives of the humanity in which we share. Without any knowledge of the man of Galilee we could never have any awareness of the majesty of the redemption from the power and rule of evil from which God has plucked us, to share in the fullness of life which we are promised for all eternity, because of the resurrection of Christ.

Moreover, the promise that the Holy Spirit would lead Mother Church into all truth has led her, step by step over the ages, to apply the revelation given us in the Incarnation to ever changing cultural situations. The whole area of bioethics is very much to the fore today, for example. The Church has the duty to proclaim in this new environment, which is global in its extent, that since the Word became flesh humankind has been given the basic tool for the handling of all these issues. (See J.F.Kilner, *Bioethics and the Future of Medicine: A Christian Appraisal*.)

In all this the Christian learns the central significance of the Incarnation in the flesh (Latin *carnis*) of Jesus Christ. The Incarnation means that the Man of Nazareth Jesus was limited by time, place, and the cultural climate of Galilee. Being only in one place at any one time, he was only able to give us samples of the power of love and of what God's saving purpose could mean for other lands and civilisations. He could only heal a 'sample' of sick folk, feed only a 'sample' of the hungry poor, and so had to pass all others by. Even in the Garden of Gethsemane, as Son of Man, he must have felt the burden of this limitation. Why must he die - and die so soon?

It was as Son of Man that he had to think in this way, appearing reluctant to assist the Syro-Phoenician woman who sought his help on the grounds that he had time and opportunity to reveal God's love only to the people of Israel. It was as Son of God, however, that he promised to send the Holy Spirit after his death (John 14:26) to "teach you everything". Even as he talked with his 'chosen' disciples they were becoming aware that he was not just 'Jesus of Nazareth', but was at the same time the incarnate Word of God. In consequence, the people of the 'chosen' community of the Resurrection could only understand the secret of the Word addressed to them when they discovered this Word to be theirs in terms of its being incarnate in their own hearts and minds.

So the new young Church, composed of all kinds of Near Eastern people united to the risen Christ by the Holy Spirit, was in reality a resurrected people in their life on earth. As such the Church can be said to be the continuation in space and time of the incarnation of the Christ who was no less than the emissary to this planet Earth of the Being of the all-holy triune God of eternity.

The Church then was not just to announce the Good News of God, it was to be, as Second Isaiah had said, the community that conveyed into the life of the world the unimaginable love of God. The Church was to take to itself the two commandments of Jesus, which he himself had taken over from the *Torah* (Deuteronomy 6:4) - they were to love God with all their heart, soul, intelligence and physical strength - in response to the fact made visible in the Incarnation that God had first loved them and their neighbours. We should in turn love our neighbours "as ourselves" (Leviticus 19:18, cited by Jesus) - this phrase could be expressed "because your neighbour wants to be loved, just as you want him to love you".

This means that we are to love our neighbours into making them love others. That may seem like asking for the moon. "With men this is impossible", said Jesus (Matthew 19:27), "but with God all things are possible", because Jesus in sending the Spirit sends him to pour out in us the love for neighbour that is in his own heart.

Yes, "your neighbour wants to be loved". Ruth Rendell, in *Heartstones* tells of a classically mad father, a scholar, who taught his brilliant young daughter a one-sided interpretation of the Greek philosophy of life. This philosophy led her to become anorexic. She succumbed to the belief that matter, in this case her body, was not the 'real', only the spirit is the 'real'. Finally, in order to enter the world of the spirit, she committed suicide. The tragedy is that she, not merely her spirit, could have been saved by love, not by the philosophy of a fanatically 'Hellenic' father.

But living the life of love is a dangerous thing to contemplate. How do we conceive of it in a world of greed and violence? The prophet who sought to 'expound' God's ways to his contemporary Jewish friends and neighbours, condemned as they were to undergo every torment of mind and spirit the human frame can undergo in Babylon's pagan and cruel social life, declares a remarkable truth of God to those who had ears to hear: "I form light and create darkness, I make weal and create woe; I the LORD do all these things" (Isaiah 45:7).

The NRSV translates the original as it does because the two words 'weal' and 'woe' produce in English an attractive assonance. But the Hebrew wording is more stark and shocking. 'Weal' is actually the word *shalom*, that wonderful Hebrew term that derives from a root meaning 'completion' or 'wholeness', even 'wholesomeness' or 'healthiness'; but it also carries the theological content of spiritual wholeness, fullness of life, satiety and peace. That, of course, sounds too good to us. On the other hand 'woe' is actually the Hebrew *ra'*, meaning evil in every sense of the term. Its sense covers both moral evil and natural calamities. And our text says that such *ra'* is of God! So strong is the Old Testament sense of the providential love and controlling power of God.

Clearly God's purpose in creating is not to produce a mechanical robotic cosmos. What about 'black holes' in outer space? Or what about whole galaxies of stars colliding with each other and then disintegrating to their 'death'? The cosmos is evidently full of development, change and conflict, and there is an evil power at work in the created world: for as Paul says in Romans 8:19-21:

> The created universe... was made subject to frustration, not of its own choice, but by the will of the one who subjected it, yet with the hope that creation itself will be set free from

its bondage to decay and obtain the glorious freedom of
God's children.

The cherubim and the seraphim, these Sphinx-like creatures
described as gods in the pagan religions of the day, and symbols of *ra*'
as they were, had been put to the service of the true God, "beneath the
feet of Yahweh". They even protect the place where his reconciling
love could be met with by all, namely, in the Holy of Holies, first in
the Tabernacle, and then in the Jerusalem Temple.

God created a humanity that is not under his dictatorship, with
the possibility of existing in whatever way it sees as good - free even
to rebel. Yet, even though a sparrow falls to the ground either
naturally or from human cruelty, it does not die "apart from your
Father" (Matthew 10:29). That is to say, God never ceases to remain
in control of what is both 'weal' and 'woe', and is always able and
willing to bring good out of evil, joy out of pain, light out of darkness,
life out of death.

That kind of world, God's kind of world, is what the individual
is baptised into in the beginning of her days. "Love conquers all",
Amor vincit omnia, uttered first by the non-Christian poet Virgil but
quoted by Chaucer the Christian, is the great promise given to all
those who find themselves thrown into the fray. Dangerous, we
said, yes, the danger of suffering pain and sorrow, enmity and
rejection, even a crown of thorns and a cruel death. But there is
also the other promise, "I will be with you, even to the end of the
world". This assurance Jesus had expressed earlier, in Hebraic
eschatological language, knowing that his kingdom would triumph;
when the 72 sent out to preach and heal returned, he exclaimed,
"I watched Satan fall from heaven like a flash of lightning" (Luke
10:18).

The individual Christian has now been made deeply aware that
what has happened to him or her is not something s/he has 'won' by
his or her own efforts. S/he now knows the reality of faith. As Karl
Barth says of Romans 5:17, the Christian

> rests in a new found assurance that he is living in covenant
> with God, that covenant which God had first bestowed
> upon him. In consequence he will not have an anxious,
> clouded, desperate life, but a royal, a sovereign life, that
> eternal life that the ever-living God has granted him as his
> partner in the covenant" (*A Shorter Commentary on Romans*
> p.56).

But faith does not ignore the possible cost of 'walking with God'. If
we follow Jesus, we will surely meet with pain and anxiety (as did
Jesus!) before love can conquer all. Paul's explanation of faith has

nothing to do with idealism or optimism. The world that we live in, the world of both humans and inanimate nature is groaning with pain, and 'walking with God' does not exempt us from sharing in that pain. However the promise of the glory that is awaiting us beckons us to accept still another gift from God, and that is the exciting power of hope; we can now see that the sufferings of this time are far outweighed by the glory to come. This 'glorification' was won for us by Jesus alone. It is promised to us in his words on the cross, "It is finished" (John 19:30), even though this 'glorification' that God had in mind was still hidden.

So when we share with Jesus the weakness, the suffering and the temptation of the humiliated Son of God, in whom Paul insisted God himself lived (2 Corinthians 5:19), we remember that the cross was followed by resurrection. Christ's future in glory is now ours as well! Nor do those (Paul continues in Romans 8:26-27) whose hope is in Christ have to wait for that future; our present waiting is already full of the 'presence', the incarnate Christ who through the Holy Spirit "helps our infirmity". Moreover, this 'presence' was all planned for each member of the covenant even "before the world was" (Ephesians 1:4).

The Incarnation was a 'one-off' event in the world's history. Yet it was anticipated "in the beginning", in the mind of God. It was further made known to us in the stories that have come to us from Patriarchal times, as when through word of promise God let there be known in 'event' his almighty power, faithfulness and constancy, in other words in 'theophanies'. In this way God actually became himself Abraham's righteousness, so that an ungodly man could be acquitted and justified by God. Thereafter God gave his promise to Moses, "I will be with you". Consequently prophets dared address the Divine as "O Immanuel, God is with us" (Isaiah 8:8), and Second Isaiah could exemplify that divine title in particular by declaring that "God is in Israel" (Isaiah 45:14, Hebrew and KJV).

The 'centre event' we know of as 'incarnation' happened at that point in human history when the Word of God became flesh and dwelt among us, full of grace and truth. Jesus is still incarnate in our human flesh because he rose and ascended in it! The "royal sovereign life" we possess, as Paul calls it, is the important event for us, for the life we live in the flesh is the very life of the risen and ascended Jesus who by the Spirit of God has taken possession of our lives in turn. Incarnation has never ceased. It cannot, and will not, because it is of the very nature of God, the "Three-in-One", to reveal himself as love and salvation for the children whom he has invited to come in and share his joy and for whom he became human, for ever. Yes, the Incarnation means that God is now forever human: he has forever bound himself to us and us to him in Jesus.

We may conclude this chapter with a summary of John Calvin's teaching, in two sentences - Calvin the great European reformer:

> The whole of humanity is represented by Christ and offered up to God, and perfected in him. Without the Incarnation this could never have happened.

The second summary statement is this:

> The whole of God dwells in the incarnate Christ. The context of this wondrous exchange that takes place in the person of Christ is given now to us in the reality of worship.

Chapter Seven

EPILOGUE

In our search for truth in any area of the mind we have to recognise that we ourselves may belong amongst the great majority of humanity who are unwitting and unacknowledged captives, perhaps even slaves, to our particular culture. Moreover, this is especially true, interestingly enough, of intellectuals working in any scholarly field of study. This is just as truly the case amongst biblical scholars as it is in any other area of scholarship.

The key issue for any one of us is to listen to the question Jesus put to his disciples: "Who do people say that the Son of Man is?", and then to ask ourselves the pointed question: "But who do you say that I am?" (Matthew 16:13-15).

For many people, scholars or otherwise, the idea of incarnation is inconceivable. Jesus the man, yes, a healer, a revolutionary, a mystic, a prophet, a rabbi, and so on, but Son of God, no! Many scholarly works have appeared in recent years by intellectuals who are simply unable to break with their dualistic, Neo-Platonic sea of thought and cultural background, and so are unable to make the answer that Peter did. In 1967 Brandon gave us a picture of Jesus as a political revolutionary. In 1978 Morton Smith depicted him as a magician. The Jewish scholar Geza Vermes, specialist in the Dead Sea Scrolls, described him in 1981 as a Galilean charismatic. Chilton, in 1984, saw him as a village rabbi. The Dead Sea Scrolls have had a fascination for some scholars. In 1985 Falk supposed him to be a member of one of the Essene communities out of which came the Scrolls. He has been followed closely by Mrs Barbara Thieling, of Sydney, Australia, who has outlined a life of Jesus for us: she suggests his teaching was affected by Essene beliefs; he did not die on the cross, having been only numbed by the vinegar handed up to him, but was resuscitated in the coolness of the tomb. Later he married Mary Magdalene and from her fathered a family of three.

Hollywood too has its ideas about Jesus. A generation ago it gave the world the spectacular *The King of Kings*. If you can remember it you know how you came away from the theatre feeling, "That is not a true picture of Jesus. It is only Hollywood's attempt to picture him".

Naturally it is impossible for a sinful human being to portray how a sinless man or woman might speak or act in any given situation. The rock opera Jesus Christ Superstar has been widely played. It is a good opera, but the Jesus played in it is not at all like the Jesus we read about in the Gospels. The portraiture in it is as out of focus as any medieval stained-glass window. And anyway it ends with his burial.

We note, however, that when Peter replied, "You are the Christ, the Son of the Living God", Jesus said to him: "Blessed are you, Simon son of Jonah! For flesh and blood [science and philosophy?] has not revealed this to you, but my Father in heaven". In other words, the old saying of Anselm still stands: "Fides Quaerens Intellectum", "Faith seeking understanding" - that is, I must begin with the 'given', and bring my own reasoning under it, if I am to understand the meaning of life and love. Even more, the Christian faith is actually a way of life itself and so cannot be attained by any detached objective reasoning.

The 'given' is the Incarnation; without it there can be no Christian theology, no Christian spirituality; where it was rejected in the early Christian centuries there flourished all kinds of heresies, Arianism, Docetism, Apollinarianism, each and all of which have surfaced in our time under new guises and been taken up by new schools of thought. In consequence we hear it declared today that we are in a post-Christian era, that this is the New Age of Man, and it requires a whole new intellectual approach if we are ever to use the word 'God' again.

In this 'postmodern' age, we have actually gone beyond a mere return to Platonism (which at least had the advantage of being a single coherent view of how things are), but have actually taken up other ancient ideas and decided that there is no longer any overarching worldview. As a result each of us may have our own faith. The logic of this position is that no one of these individual faiths is right. It is virtually a declaration (usually made quite unwittingly) that there must only be a pluralist approach to reality. The result is that a belief in pluralism has actually become the new religion in itself, despite the widely held view that all individual searches for truth are 'valid for me', even if, perchance, they are not right.

Consequently we are told to respect and not deride all those who dabble with Zen, then try Confucianism, take refuge in Buddhism or Indian mysticism, or else in one of the Western cults that have invaded us from the East, such as Theosophy, Spiritualism, Voodooism, Anthroposophy, Astrology, even the examination of the human anatomy and psyche; from the latter it is said there arises a hedonic nativism, perhaps described as 'the alternative lifestyle', shown in the sexual revolution, or more radically and specifically in the pursuit of money, power, acclamation - all aspects of the New Age wearing its multifarious and fissiparous face in any and all of these 'new religions' (See Lesslie Newbigin: *The Gospel in a Pluralist Society*).

What we have in 'New Age Man' is the unwitting, individualistic, greedy male or female, pursuing today's 'enlightened' equivalent to Jesus' declaration: "He who seeks to save his soul will lose it". (See Paul's way of expressing the above at 2 Corinthians 4:4). For s/he is centred upon a private and selfish pursuit for a spiritual meaning to life, some kind of private inner light. Actually, it would seem, s/he is seeking escape from what we saw in the previous chapter, the dangerous and exacting business of loving.

Such were the desires of Schopenhauer, Heine, Amial of a past generation, or of W.B. Yeats, who longed to retreat to "the lake island of Innisfree in a Celtic twilight"! Not for him the earthy, materialistic concern for social justice for the millions of the simple poor whose whole existence is dominated by the pressing need to find the bare necessities sufficient to feed and clothe their miserable family. These basic needs of the human race are not 'spiritual' enough to distract modern intellectual man from his or her search for 'God', or 'meaning' in this chaotic world!

In its extreme forms, what we are describing therefore is the appearance of a new super-spirituality such as claims that all material aspects of life are intrinsically inferior and even wicked. (See Francis A. Schaeffer, *The New Super-Spirituality*, pp.20-21). Thus:

> Only the so-called 'spiritual' realm should be accepted as the sphere of God's activity, only the soul matters, it must be served, so that it can go to heaven.

In such a case the result is that the 'person' disappears; only the soul is valuable, and its value discernible only in terms of 'spirit'.

There is, however, one way out. The 'transcendental agnostic' (cf. Brad Stetson, *Pluralism and Particularity in Religious Belief*, pp.7,11), has probably never heard of H.R. Mackintosh's trenchant statement in his *The Christian Apprehension of God*: "All religious knowledge of God, wherever existing, comes by revelation; otherwise we should be committed to the incredible position that man can know God without his willing to be known". We can know God, in other words, only because he wills to be known and has willed to be known in the Incarnation of Jesus.

What we must bear in mind is that no amount of speculation that avoids revelation through incarnation can reveal to us the creative suffering of God. Those who reject and scorn the idea that the divine Being suffers (!) have not listened to the agonised contention of those who have faced up to the Incarnation. The fatal flaw in the many 'Hellenic' propositions about God is its *hubris*, intellectual pride, the imagined ability of creatures to understand their Creator, and actually dictate what the Creator can or cannot do! They suggest there is no realm of mystery. Incarnation is the reverse. It involves "the expansive creativity of loving self-limitation" (Alan E. Lewis, *The Burial of God* p.355).

It is often thought to be axiomatic that God cannot suffer, but the Incarnation reveals that he desires and chooses to do so in passionate loving concern to redeem his creation; and do we not see him actually doing so particularly in the Cross of Christ? (Ulrich Simon, *Atonement from Holocaust to Paradise* p.134)

The modern secularist may jibe at the Jew or Christian, declaring: "Your religious experience is only illusion, it is a type of hallucination, it belongs in the dream world and is just a projection from the subconscious". The answer is, of course, that religious experience can be described in physiological terms - involving the brain, the nervous ssystem and so on. But this kind of description is only 'one side of the coin', as it tells us nothing about the content of the experience, and whether it is based on what is true. Neuro-science cannot tell us what is on the back of the coin - only faith, and faith is a gift from God which can only be tested in two ways:

(a) does it correspond to what has been revealed of God in Incarnation, and witnessed to by his people?

(b) does it bear good fruit in the life of the person who claims such an experience?

The modern world is simply intimidated by science, whether in the area of astro-physics or psychology. Perhaps we should say, intimidated by 'experts', as the true scientist is humble about the extent of human knowledge. Here is an example in the sphere of the scientific study of language. The Postmodernist declares that since human languages are always changing we cannot believe the biblical affirmation that "The Word of the Lord stands for ever". But because she also claims that 'god' can be sought only in the realm of the spirit, she misses the point made in Chapter Four that once the Word became flesh in Christ it became a fixture, an absolute, one that cannot be moved. How we interpret him in our human language is another matter, but he remains fixed as the Centre.

Michael Polanyi has had some helpful things to say about the relation of language to meaning. There is no meaning without the physical expression of sounds or marks on paper or screen, but you cannot reduce meaning to those sounds or marks. There are different levels of communication - sounds, syllables, words, grammar, meaning. Each level specifies the higher level, but does not control it. Each level specifies the boundaries within which the higher level should operate, but leaves freedom within those boundaries. The higher level in each case introduces entirely new principles. You cannot reduce a higher level to a lower level. Or in terms of the dialogue with platonic thought - without a body, there is no soul, but you cannot reduce soul to body. (Drusilla Scott, *Michael Polanyi*, formerly *Everyman Revisited*)

We have to make our 'interpretation', then, plain in the languages and cultures of this world, even across the generation gap, even between the rich and poor, the East and West, in terms of the ordinary outlook of people concerned about unemployment, politics, economics, prisons, income tax, none of which seem to have any place in the spiritual life - or of the double demand of Christ, to love God wholly, and to love our neighbour, if necessary, painfully. This has been exhibited particularly through the relationship of covenant, from which God's people then learn to live in covenant with one another (Walter Brueggemann, *In Man we Trust*). In the meantime I can only hope that the following statement of a theologian a generation ago could not have been written today: "Jesus' thinking is plebeian thinking, and is not academically respectable, in that it is too earthy." This theologian later turned his mind to study 'secular theology'!

What we must all learn or relearn is that the Bible is so far from being a collection of myths that it might even be entitled "The History of God". For God so involves himself in space and time that the whole 'story of God', concrete actions in the history of Israel, can legitimately be called his history.

The Jewish people were the first to make this affirmation, while keeping their feet firmly on the ground. At Exodus 4:31 we read: "Israel believed in the LORD and in his servant Moses". As such it is not an exposition of who or what God is in his essential Being, rather it is a report about what the unknown God has been doing down the ages, through such as Moses and his like. Thus in the Bible we discover that God is a God in search of man. In a book with that very title, *God in Search of Man*, Abraham J. Heschel, the warmly regarded Jewish scholar, writes: "The fact is that prophetic revelation was not merely an act of experience but an act of being experienced" (p. 230).

These words lead me to close this "Theology of the Incarnation" in an unusual manner. My wording may reveal my own complete assurance that Heschel is right. It is customary for an author to include a few words of dedication to a special friend or dear one after the title page right at the beginning of his book. Instead of this, I choose here at the end of mine to give a few words of dedication to the memory of my very dear wife, Nancy. In her final months of painful and distressing cancer, when she bravely warred against the distressful psychological side-effects of the medical treatment, she exhibited that convoluted mixture of love (in the sense of *hesed*), joy (in the sense of exhilaration), and peace (in the sense of *shalom*), which is the sacramental experience (in the sense of *pele'*) that God grants to his dying loved ones. She had been so aware of the reality of the resurrection of Jesus and of his love and presence with her in this life here and now, that she could look through death and know that she would share in the resurrection life of Jesus herself and so be raised from the dead. In this manner, she and all the faithful are given a foretaste of the glory that is awaiting us 'on the other side'.

Index of Hebrew and Greek words
explained on the page where they first occur

Relevant Bibliography

Achtemeier, Paul J. and Elizabeth, *The Old Testament Roots of our Faith*, Peabody, MA, Hendrikson Publishers, revised ed., 1995

Baeck, Leo, *The Essence of Judaism*, 1963

Balz and Schneider (ed.), *Exegetical Dictionary of the New Testament*, Grand Rapids, Eerdmans, vol.1 1990, vol.2 1991, vol.3 1993 - article by H.Ritt in vol.2

Barker, Eileen, *New Religious Movements: A Perspective for Understanding Society*, New York and Toronto, Edwin Mellen Press, 1982

Barth, Karl, *A Shorter Commentary on Romans*, SCM Press 1959 and 1963

Barth, Karl, *Church Dogmatics* vol.3, e.t. T. & T. Clark, Edinburgh 1961

Bouquet, A.C., *The Christian Faith and Non-Christian Religions*, 1959

Beeby, H.D., *Grace Abounding: Hosea, International Theological Commentary*, Grand Rapids, Eerdmans and Edinburgh, Handsel Press, 1989

Bietenhard, Hans, *Jesus and Metraton*, in *Die Himmlische Welt im Urchristentum und Spätjudentum*, Tubingen: Mohr/Siebeck, 1951

Boaz, Frank, *The History of Anthropology*, 1904

Brooks, R. and Collins J.J. (eds), *Hebrew Bible or Old Testament? : Studying the Bible in Judaism and Christianity* in *Christianity and Judaism in Antiquity 5*, Indiana, University of Notre Dame Press, 1990

Brueggemann, Walter, *In Man We Trust*, Atlanta, John Knox Press, 1972

Clark, Stephen R.L., *From Athens to Jerusalem: The Love of Wisdom and the Love of God*, Oxford, Clarendon Press, 1984

Cobb, John B. Jr, *The Resurrection of the Soul*, HTR, April 1987

Cooke, S.A., *The Old Testament, a Reinterpretation*, 1936

Cooper, John W., *Body, Soul and Life Everlasting: Biblical Anthropology and the Monism-Dualism Debate*, Grand Rapids, Eerdmans, 1989

Cornford, Francis MacDonald, *The Republic of Plato*, OUP, 1941

Cullman, O., Wolfson, W.A., Jaeger, W. and Cadbury, H.J., *Immortality and Resurrection. Four Essays*, "Ingersoll Lectures", New York, Macmillan, 1965

Eichrodt, Walter, *Theology of the Old Testament Vols. 1 and 2*, London, SCM Press, 1967

Eissfeldt, Otto., *Introduction to the Old Testament*, Blackwell, 1965

Capon, R.F., *The Romance of the Word*, Eerdmans, 1995

Frend, W.H.C., *The Rise of Christianity*, Philadelphia, Fortress Press, Pa, 1984

Fretheim, Terence E., *The Suffering of God: An Old Testament Perspective*, "Overtures to Biblical Theology" Vol 14. Philadelphia Pa, Fortress Press, 1984

Glasson, T. Francis, *2 Corinthians v.1-10 versus Platonism*, SJTh Vol 43, No 2, 1990

Griffith, Paul J. ed., *Christianity through Non-Christian Eyes*, Maryknoll, Orbis Books, 1990

Hallman, John M., *The Descent of God: Divine Suffering in History and Theology*, Philadelphia Pa, Fortress Press, 1991

Heschel, Abraham Joshua, *God in Search of Man: A Philosophy of Judaism*, Harper and Row 1955 and 1962

Higgins, A.J.B., *The Son of Man in the teaching of Jesus*, CUP 1980

Jewish Encyclopedia, Vol 11, article on *Shekinah*, by Blau, Funk and Wagnall's Company, New York and London, 1905

Johnson, A.R., *The One and the Many*, University of Wales Press, 1942

Kilner, J.F., *Bioethics and the Future of Medicine: A Christian Appraisal*, Eerdmans 1995

Kitamori, Kozoh, *The Theology of the Pain of God*, London, SCM Press, 1966

Knight, G.A.F., *From Moses to Paul: A Christological Study in the Light of our Hebraic Heritage*, London, Lutterworth Press, 1949

Knight, G.A.F., *A Biblical Approach to the Doctrine of the Trinity*, SJTh Occas. Papers no 1 1953 and 1958 (now T. & T.Clark, Edinburgh)

Knight, G.A.F., *The New Israel: Isaiah 56-66, International Theological Commentary*, Edinburgh, Handsel Press and Grand Rapids, Eerdmans, 1985

Knight, G.A.F., *Israel, the Land and Resurrection*, in "The Witness of the Jews to God" ed. Torrance, David W., Edinburgh, Handsel Press, 1982

Knight, G.A.F., *Is 'Righteousness' Right?*, SJTh Vol 41, No 1, 1988

Knight, G.A.F., *Revelation of God: Song of Songs and Jonah, International Theological Commentary*, Edinburgh, Handsel Press and Grand Rapids, Eerdmans 1988

Koester, Helmut, *History, Culture, and Religion of the Hellenistic Age*, second ed. 1995

Lacocque, André, *Israel, Pierre de touche de l'oecumenisme*, Verbum Caro, 48, 1958

Lawson, John, *The Biblical Theology of St Irenaeus*, Epworth, 1948

Lapide, Pinchas and Moltmann, Jurgen, *Jewish Monotheism and Christian Trinitarian Doctrine*, Philadelphia Pa, Fortress Press, 1979

Lapide, Pinchas and Moltmann, Jurgen, *The Resurrection of Jesus: A Jewish Perspective*, SPCK & Augsburg, 1983

Leon-Dufour, Xavier, *Life and Death in the New Testament*, San Francisco, Harper and Row, 1986

Lewis, Alan E., *The Burial of God*, SJTh Vol 40 no 3, 1987

Lindars, Barnabas SSF, *Jesus Son of man: A Fresh Examination of the Son of Man Sayings in the Gospels in the Light of Recent Research*, SPCK 1983

Mackintosh, H.R., *The Christian Apprehension of God*, SCM Press 1929

Macquarrie, John, *Mary for all Christians*, Grand Rapids, Eerdmans, 1990 and London, Collins, 1991

Marmorstein, A., *The Old Rabbinic Doctrine of God, I The Name and Attributes of God*, 1927

Michaeli, Frank, *L'Ancien Testament et L'Eglise Chretienne d'Aujourd'hui*, 1957

G.F.Moore, *Intermediaries in Jewish Theology*, HTR, 1922

Moses, A.D.A., *Matthew's Transfiguration Story and Jewish Christian Controversy*, Sheffield Academic Press, 1996

Murtonen, Almo, *The Figure of Metatron*, VT3, 1953

Newbigin, Lesslie, *The Gospel in a Pluralist Society*, Grand Rapids, Eerdmans, and Geneva, WCC Publications, 1989

Oden, Thomas C., *The Living God*, San Francisco, Harper & Row, 1987

Oden, Thomas C., *Requiem: A Lament in Three Movements*, Nashville, Abingdon Press, 1995

Parker, T.H.L., *The Doctrine of the Knowledge of God, a study in the theology of John Calvin*, Oliver and Boyd 1952

Quispel, Gilles, *Gnosticism and the New Testament*, Verbum Caro, 19, 1965

Reid, J., Newbigin L., and Pullinger, D., *Modern, Postmodern and Christian*, Lausanne Occasional Paper, Edinburgh, Handsel 1997

Rendell, Ruth, *Headstones*, a Hutchinson Novella, 1987

Roberts, J.J.M., *The Davidic Origin of the Zion Tradition*, J.B.L. 92, No 3, Sept 1973

Samuelson, Herbert, *That the God of the Philosophers is not the God of Abraham, Isaac and Jacob*, HTR, Jan. 1972

Sandmel, Samuel, *Philo of Alexandria*, Oxford, 1979

Schaeffer, Francis, *The New Super-Spirituality*, Hodder 1973

Scott, Drusilla, *Michael Polanyi*, Harper Collins 1997

Segal, Alan, *"Ruler of this World"*, in Jewish and Christian Self-Definition, London, SCM Press pp. 245-68, 1981

Simon, Ulrich, *Atonement from Holocaust to Paradise*, London, James Clarke 1987

Spong, J.S., *Resurrection - Myth or Reality*, San Francisco, Harper Collins, 1994

Stetson, Brad, *Pluralism and Particularity in Religious Belief*, Westport Conn., Praeger, 1994

Stroumsa, Gedaliahu, *Form(s) of God: Some Notes on Metatron and Christ*, HTR, pp.269-88, 1983

Taylor, A.E., *Plato, the Man and his Work*, London, Methuen & Co., 1926

Terrien, Samuel L., *The Elusive Presence*, San Francisco, Harper & Row, 1978

Torrance, D.W. (ed.) *The Witness of the Jews to God*, Edinburgh, Handsel 1982

Wallis, R.T., *Neoplatonism*, London, Duckworth, 1972